MASTERING IN-HOUSE SEO

SECOND EDITION

BLEEDING EDGE STRATEGIES AND TACTICS
FROM LEADING IN-HOUSE SEO EXPERTS

BlueArray
We stand for SEO.

PUBLISHED AND COMPILED BY

SIMON SCHNIEDERS

FOUNDER OF BLUE ARRAY

Mastering In-House SEO 2021 Edition - Bleeding Edge Strategies And Tactics From Leading In-House SEO Experts

ISBN 9781916883918

Published in June 2021

This book is dedicated
to the incredible team at
Blue Array

Simon Schnieders

PRAISE FOR MASTERING IN-HOUSE SEO

"If you're looking to drive results internally this book is for you. Packed full of snippets covering all aspects of SEO it's aimed at helping you not only learn more but also tips to get stuff done."

KEVIN WILES
Group SEO Manager, Halfords

"The only book that really addresses the struggles in-house SEO specialists deal with. Not only is it invaluable for anyone with an in-house SEO role, but it provides those working agency-side with unique insights into the challenges in-house SEO specialists face."

STEVEN VAN VESSUM
VP of Community, ContentKing

"With a great mix of contributors with varied experience, I found it a really enjoyable read. A must-have for any in-house or agency marketer"

DAVID WILLIAMS
Senior SEO Manager, Jellyfish

"Creating the buy-in you need to be successful as an SEO within a large organization can be tricky at best. That's why I highly recommend this book with real tips from real in-house SEOs."

MORDY OBERSTEIN
Head of Communications, Semrush

"Being an in-house SEO guy is always exciting and tricky at the same time. This book will help you ensure your success in the long-run."

DIMITRIS DRAKATOS
SEO & ASO Lead, Peanut

"Whether you're making the transition from an agency to in-house SEO, or just looking to stay ahead of the trend, this book is an invaluable resource. It's a great mixture of case studies to inspire new ideas and guidance to help you overcome imposter syndrome."

DANIEL RAWLEY
SEO Specialist - International and Start-ups,
Twinkl Educational Publishing

"This book is a breakthrough in the industry for sure. It gives you an invaluable viewpoint of other in-house SEO professionals just like you. Learn about their struggles and successes and enjoy the read."

ROMAN SADOWSKI
SEO Account Manager, Iprospect

"Mastering in-house SEO in 2021 is a lot more complicated than many think. This book doesn't just dive deep, it brings real life examples from real in-house SEOs. Of course, agencies and consultants who often work with large online organizations will learn from it as well. Don't miss it."

IGAL STOLPNER
Former VP Growth & SEO, Investing.com

CONTENTS

FOREWORD

After the enormous success of the first Mastering In-House SEO, which became an Amazon bestseller, we're delighted to be back with a comprehensive new edition, where we hear from both old friends and new.

We like to say that we 'do it as a team' here at Blue Array – and this year, whether thinking about getting this project out into the world, or about the world more broadly – these words have become particularly meaningful, we think.

Anyone working in this space will know that a year is a long time in digital marketing – but, given that since we last collected the latest thinking in our field, the COVID-19 pandemic has swept the world – this one has been, to say the least, exceptional.

We know many people's 'office' is now the kitchen table, the spare room or the sofa, and as such, we've never seen customers get such a profound shove into the world of online shopping. And this has prompted practical creativity from everyone, from those working in the travel industry to educational publishing, which you can find out more about in this new edition.

The past 12 months have been tragic in so many ways, but lots of you have kept turning up every single day to continue to support your brand's success, and many people we've spoken to have done just that and more.

Collaboration is a core principle at Blue Array, and this year, it feels like everyone has had to put in much more work to get things done with colleagues, who are not only in different parts of the business, but may be in different timezones, on different continents.

Technical know-how and producing quality content are both core areas for skills development if you want a successful, long-term career in this rewarding space. Something that shouldn't just be possible, but desirable too. And several of our writers have shared frank advice for making this a reality.

But it's people that a lot of us have been missing during this time – and it's people who are our customers and our champions when it comes to SEO.

Whether looking inside the business, at getting support from the right colleagues or educating your stakeholders, or outside, to the people who've arrived at your website, doing the work of education is a commitment we should all make, if we want to see SEO lead business through this latest transition.

And, as several of our authors make clear, SEO can lead businesses to greater things, whether you're the first SEO person through the door, or you're joining a huge global team.

This is not a 'dark art', this isn't anything secret or too complex, this is a worthwhile profession and an important part of any business, and in the following pages you'll find many meaningful expressions of these facts.

As the Founder of the UK's largest specialist SEO agency I feel a unique responsibility to elevate our people, our customers and our industry. We've recently rebranded to say at Blue Array that 'We stand for SEO' and this book I hope serves, in part, that stance.

Simon Schnieders

Founder of Blue Array

simon@bluearray.co.uk

THINKING LIKE A JOURNALIST – AND AN SEO – TO MAKE CONTENT 'QUEEN'

NICOLA AGIUS

SEO DIRECTOR, JUNGLE CREATIONS

In 2020, Nicola completed something of a career odyssey, having started off as a journalist for places like The Daily Mirror, The Sun and OK! magazine, before becoming full-time SEO Director at Jungle Creations, a London-based digital media company that operates themed channels, such as VT, Twisted and Four Nine.

Skilled in SEO, but also adept at the technical skills, such as statistical data analysis, Nicola is adamant that everything she does is informed by her journalistic and content-writing experience.

I work specifically in SEO news – so I'm not trying to get a product to rank well – I'm trying to get news stories and blogs to rank instead.

Perhaps you think this means that what I have to say won't be immediately relevant. But I strongly believe it's relevant to all SEOs.

Google often tells us that the first things we should think about are content and user intent. But the industry is still very much focussed on mechanics, and not enough on the SEO's responsibility to the reader. This is why I try to practise what I call 'journalistic SEO'.

Of course, you need to have everything in place from a technical perspective. But one of the reasons I believe so strongly in journalistic SEO is because of my experience at The Sun.

EXPLAINING WHY NOT TO WRITE 'WHO IS KAT SLATER IN EASTENDERS?'

Even someone who has never read the paper will know The Sun is famous for its exclusive celebrity content.

The website gets a lot of direct traffic from loyal readers who visit daily, specifically for its showbiz stories. So you may be surprised to learn that for a while, the website's soap (opera) content was underperforming on Google.

Why was that? When you come from a purely SEO background, you have an instinct to jampack headlines with keywords – which of course is fantastic for visibility. But what's the point in ranking on Google if that doesn't translate into clicks?

The Sun is iconic for its fun and engaging headlines. Just because we are writing with Google in mind, that doesn't mean our headlines and content should suffer. This is where journalistic SEO comes in.

At The Sun, we had an editorial team dedicated to writing evergreen features for SEO called 'explainers'. But we didn't have the right strategy when it came to soaps.

Instead of thinking about user intent, we were focusing too much on keywords. So we ended up with explainers with headlines like 'Who is Kat Slater in EastEnders?'. This didn't work.

Think about what kind of person is going to Google characters in soaps like Kat Slater. It's EastEnders fans. And EastEnders fans are not going to Google 'Who is Kat Slater' – because she's been on the show for more than 20 years.

Even people who aren't EastEnders fans have probably heard of her. So why would anyone click on this story?

If Kat Slater is trending, then yes, we should write up a story – but not about who she is. I understand that we'll need 'Kat Slater' and 'EastEnders' in the headline, and that it needs to be evergreen, but a flat explainer is just not going to be read.

So I put a complete stop to this practice.

Fans are much more interested in upcoming storylines – for example, if she's going to be in a big car crash in Friday's episode. So a much more engaging headline would be, 'Will Kat Slater die in EastEnders on Friday?'.

THINK LIKE A JOURNALIST – AND AN SEO

Similar rules apply for liveblogs. At one point, I was overseeing the SEO of a 'Love Island' liveblog for The Sun. It dominated Google all evening and the page views were fantastic – so much so that, at one point, this article accounted for 40 percent of all traffic to the website.

One of the techniques I used here was to keep updating the headline depending on what was happening in real-time – you've got to make sure headlines focus on what's happening right now. You need to think like a journalist, while applying SEO best practice.

What I learned at The Sun is that content and site quality should never suffer as a result of using keywords. You've always got to make a copy interesting, because it's still got to be read. If it's not, you'll have a high bounce rate.

And remember, if you're working in news SEO, your publication is a business that relies on your content performing well, not just being visible to an algorithm.

Sometimes I still can't believe I am an SEO Director – with a degree in journalism, and having spent my entire career working as a reporter and editor.

I didn't know that crossing over into SEO was an option, so I think I'm very lucky. But to get to where I am now, I've had to prove myself, taking on hard, technical SEO problems like site migrations – and acquiring a lot of new skills along the way.

Over the past few years, time after time, something has become really evident to me – while on-page optimisation is important – I have always found the key to winning search traffic is to put the reader first and produce high-quality, original content. Even if you're creating something to target specific search queries, that should never mean the copy is any less readable.

I've also learned that there isn't a 'one size fits all' solution when it comes to SEO. When I started my last role prior to Jungle Creations, at Entertainment Daily, it became evident very quickly that this site didn't have the same level of authority as The Sun.

So I had to rethink my editorial strategy – but I am delighted to say that after a change in tactics – search traffic doubled in three months. Here's the short version.

We were struggling to rank for single keywords (for example 'EastEnders'). We simply didn't have the authority to rank for just the title of a TV show, because we could not compete with bigger publications.

So I decided to concentrate on targeting long-tail search queries instead. To figure out what those queries might be, I started watching previews of shows and began asking myself, as a viewer, 'okay, while I'm watching this, what would I Google?'.

We then started writing features targeting specific questions we thought might come up. So, for example, BBC One's 'The A Word' is a great show about a little boy with autism, and one of the biggest search queries was whether the actor has autism in real life.

We wrote a feature targeting that search query and the article performed brilliantly. In fact, for the first time in Entertainment Daily's history, search traffic was outperforming social.

OPTIMISE FOR SEO, NOT SOCIAL, FOR THE LONG-TERM

News publishers will notice that it's often social media driving traffic to a top-performing page in real time – but that surge is usually short-lived.

While a piece of SEO evergreen content probably won't be the best-performing article on your site at any given minute, there's a good chance it'll be your top article at the end of the month.

I first noticed this pattern whilst working at Digital Spy. Although reporters would bring in fantastic exclusives that would rocket to the top of Google Analytics, at the end of the month, it was usually an SEO explainer, like 'When does Game of Thrones series 6 start' that would be the top story. SEO is definitely a long-term strategy, but it can deliver incredible results.

Having worked for a number of national newspaper and magazine websites, I know that historically, the industry has been heavily reliant on social media for traffic.

It's not a good idea to solely depend on the likes of Facebook to bring in your readers. If you get a strike against you, or if there's an algorithm change, your traffic can plummet – and it can take a while to recover.

My advice is to never put all of your eggs in one basket. And that applies to any business, not just those in publishing.

I think SEO is a fantastic career – and I'm so glad I made the jump. I'm also grateful for the training I got in creating compelling content for SEO.

In my opinion, content isn't 'king'... it's 'queen'.

HOW TO ACCESS BEST PRACTICE AND CAREER SUPPORT AT THE SAME TIME

We all know that SEO is a constantly evolving industry (thanks Google!). This means that it's crucial that SEOs take responsibility for staying up-to-date with industry news, training and more.

When you run an in-house SEO department, your company won't do this for you, so you will have to do it yourself. I've had to learn tools like Advanced Web Ranking and Semrush on my own – and a little help from YouTube of course.

If you are serious about SEO, you have to accept there's always going to be that on-the-job, self-directed training aspect.

Like a lot of in-house SEOs, I am not part of a big team. But I am part of some great groups on Facebook that are fantastic, like Women in Tech SEO, and Sisters in SEO. They're so supportive.

I also closely follow brands like Blue Array on social media. I really applauded how, during lockdown, they offered the SEO Manager Certification course for free. I passed the course and proudly have the diploma published on my LinkedIn profile, and I recommend the course. In addition, I have a copy of last year's Mastering In-House SEO book.

Finally, there are some great, and genuinely inspiring, SEO influencers I get value from following. Of course, there's the SEO legend Barry Schwartz, who always stresses the importance of creating good content so Google will rank it.

Here are some other useful people to follow:

- Kristina Azarenko
- Aleyda Solis
- Areej AbuAli
- Izzi Smith
- John Mueller
- Martin Splitt

WHAT'S HOLDING WOMEN BACK IN SEO?

Following on from conversations I've had with fellow female SEOs, there seems to be a confidence issue impacting women in our industry.

According to Moz, men on average charge 66.7 percent more than women for SEO projects (or an $8,750 median fee versus $2,250). That's a ridiculous difference. Why don't we think our time is as valuable?

In the UK, women make up just a quarter of SEOs. In Search Engine Journal's 2019 list of the '140 most influential SEOs to follow', a mere 36 women were named.

Commenting on why more women aren't on panels at SEO exhibitions, SES Conference and Expo manager Laura Roth said there are simply more applications from men.

So again, we're brought back to this issue of women SEOs perhaps lacking confidence. I personally think a lot of women who work in SEO have quiet battles with 'imposter syndrome' – it's time we address this so we can start taking action.

My advice is to network with other women as much as you can to build your confidence – even outside office hours. And when an opportunity arises, grab it. If we want to progress, we've got a responsibility to take it for ourselves.

HERE'S WHAT HAPPENS WHEN THE SEO TEAM RUNS YOUR COMPANY'S WEBSITE – PERFECT CONTENT WITH A DIRECT COMMERCIAL IMPACT

FABRIZIO BALLARINI

HEAD OF ORGANIC ACQUISITION, WISE

After starting out as an SEO Specialist, and working for major brands at Ogilvy & Mather UK, Fabrizio came on board at Wise (formerly TransferWise) as Head of Organic Growth and SEO in 2015.

Here he discusses why SEO is both so central to what his company does, and what's their approach to driving organic growth.

At Wise, we think we've built something very useful – a way to properly assess the value of website pages. We can do this for our own pages and those of our partners.

This means we have all the commercial and ranking data for clusters of keywords relevant to our industry – so if we create a page targeting a certain subset of keywords, we can predict relatively accurately how much it's going to be worth to us.

It also means we have a great way to track the value of our SEO activities at Wise and we can plan where to invest resources.

Our process consists of using various ranking APIs to scrape Search Engine Results Pages (SERP) for a couple of million keywords in our space. We have a list that's always growing as we automatically inject new keywords via Search Console API and our affiliate partners' data.

Then, we reverse engineer the 'value' of pages that show up in these results, based on whether they are websites that we own, or are websites we're partnered with.

We do additional scraping on websites to figure out if they mention us, if they link to us, if they are an affiliate partner – whether we need them to become an affiliate partner – or even if, perhaps, we should acquire them.

When it comes to long-form content, our content team now produces articles for the blog that come with an accompanying data point that tells us how many users this article is going to drive to the business. This can be done with a decent level of accuracy.

You could say this is no different from tracking ranking in traditional SEO, where you try to understand what your share of Google results is, for a certain type of keywords. The difference here is that:

a) we track something like a couple of million keywords organised by 300+ clusters and ad hoc categories relevant to us.

b) we track all the websites that show up for each of these keywords.

We also perform a bunch of other checks and tracking to determine the value of a page in case they're from web properties not owned by us. That means we basically use every keyword for our website, and supplement that with all the keywords of our partners and other websites in our space.

If you buy a tool like Semrush, it will give you some competitive history of what your industry is, which is great, but Semrush can't track the entire keyword universe across all verticals. That's why we built our own proprietary tools, allowing us to go in much deeper, on our own verticals.

Everything we do, whether that's new pages or new partnerships, should be informed by this data – whether we're doing these checks on a daily, weekly, monthly basis.

It is certainly a lot of work, but it means we've got to the point where, for our industry, we have a very in-depth, specific universe of keywords.

SEO DATA FOR SMART CONTENT CREATION

Our SEO team owns the website, from content, design, commercial optimisation, analytics, everything. That means every page is our responsibility.

We produce 500 pieces of content per quarter in 14 languages. Ordinarily, if you tell 20 editors, each of whom has got 10 freelancers on their books, to come up with content, you will end up with the same content you already have, or perhaps content you don't need. Wise is avoiding that, as our SEO data is helping us be far more precise about what articles to commission.

And so, because we are getting so much better at predicting what to do, and knowing what works and what doesn't, before, if we wrote ten articles, we might get to five that work. Now we only have to build five articles. Although this resource doesn't directly generate growth for the business, it means far greater efficiency, so in some ways, it does.

The real challenge is not only doing good SEO, but doing it at the speed that we need to create pages and get them out there. You can be doing

'perfect' SEO, but if you only publish two pages a month, you are not going to become the BBC or the Guardian, it doesn't work like that.

To get a very large footprint on the web, the speed at which we release content that is optimised and SEO-friendly is way more important to us than looking at what Google might do, in terms of an algorithm change, tomorrow.

If you are inspired to do something like this for your brand, I'd advise you to start working with ranking APIs, first. Then you're going to start building a database to store all that, together with a visualisation tool like Looker.

And once you start monitoring, you will start building data on your real share of the market, and you'll know how much each page is worth, in terms of the overall share of clicks it gets in search results.

You can go more in-depth with that valuable data using additional checks. For example, we layer page revenue with any kind of KPIs that we are measuring against these pages. We automate a lot of checks to try and understand what the real opportunity is, and we do this across millions of pages for hundreds and thousands of websites.

Having such data also means we can be really focused on our commercial impact. We don't need to do a case study that shows how fancy we may look as a result of a new Google algorithm change – because that's not important.

SEO IN CONTEXT – HOW TO GET CUSTOMERS INTERESTED IN SOMETHING THEY DON'T KNOW THEY NEED YET

What Wise does as a core service is money transfer. It's true that we provide multiple additional services, such as enterprise payment products, multi-currency accounts and cards, but the core of what we do is money transfer as a consumer service.

The problem we have with SEO that's perhaps different from other industries is that there's not enough search demand out there.

It's harder to run Google AdWords than for us to do SEO, because we're competing with banks, who tend to have hidden fees on international transfers for decades and often build perceptions that their service doesn't have a cost for its customers. So, if you think a service is free, why search for a cheaper way to do it?

If you want to get a mortgage, you're never going to do that without consulting multiple experts and price comparison sites, but that doesn't happen in money transfer, so there aren't enough keywords to optimise against.

That means our effort is not just about ranking for high-intent transactional keywords. Actually, that's just the tip of the iceberg. The challenge is being present in the entire finance vertical and explaining to users how to compare others against our proposition.

Because of this, we invest a lot in price comparison and educating customers about their existing providers, so they understand price and consider shopping for alternatives.

In practical terms, we can't just build a bunch of landing pages for money transfer and that's that. We really need to own the space, because if we don't tap into the consumer when they're not searching for us, we don't have the opportunity to tell them they need us.

This means we have to be writing content for people that might need to transfer money in a year's time, otherwise we have no chance to tell them that, when they are finally ready, that they should shop around and compare prices of different providers.

That's why SEO is becoming an increasingly important part of our marketing mix – and that needs to continue – SEO is essential for our brand. Additionally, the more we drop our price for our customers, the more we need to acquire them organically, as opposed to paid acquisition channels.

We're very fortunate that our leadership understands that creating useful content and products for our customers takes time and effort, because the return on this type of marketing is particularly good if measured in the long run.

When new people come on board, we find they're used to having to justify why SEO is a good idea and having someone else deciding if they could go ahead. At Wise, that isn't a problem, because we give teams the autonomy to experiment and take bold bets in order to drive long-term, sustainable growth.

That's quite important, because the risk is that you let leadership, who are not close to the problem, define what risks to take and you end up investing in short-term, impact marketing activities that don't really drive long-term growth.

If you want to be a website that scales from a few hundred visits to millions a month, you need to spend years and years relentlessly building valuable content to achieve that.

HOW 'STARTUP THINKING' WON BIG AT THIS $6 BILLION COMPANY

AARON BAREFOOT

GLOBAL SEO LEAD, LONDON STOCK EXCHANGE GROUP (FORMERLY REFINITIV)

Aaron joined the London Stock Exchange Group after completing an 18-month contract leading a major brand launch at sister company Refinitiv.

With a background in both agency and in-house SEO, he shares some of the key learnings he picked up from that billion-dollar transformation project.

Refinitiv officially launched in October 2018 (it was formerly known as Thomson Reuters Financial & Risk), and is one of the world's largest providers of financial-markets data and infrastructure.

It serves more than 40,000 institutions in almost every country in the world, providing data and insights, and technology and trading platforms, for the global financial-markets community.

After Thomson Reuters sold a majority of the company to investment firm Blackstone Group, in August 2019, Refinitiv was then acquired by the London Stock Exchange Group, creating a major, global, UK-headquartered financial-markets infrastructure provider.

We had huge market loyalty to our old identity, including a highly authoritative domain that had generated three straight years of strong, organic-traffic growth.

So, with a new name and new owners when Blackstone first came on board, in effect, I was working for a $6 billion startup that no one knew about yet.

That meant we had to take on the ultimate SEO challenge, of migrating to a brand-new domain, effectively launching a new financial-service brand, while continuing to improve SEO performance at a global scale.

I managed to achieve this with no significant agency help, as an SEO specialist assisted by just one junior member of staff, within a 20,000-person company.

We are seeing great results, but we had a lot of pressure to get there, because Refinitiv's new investors were a private equity firm that was expecting quick returns.

We were also expected to compete as effectively as the old brand had with firms such as Bloomberg and websites that have been around for more than 20 years. So, I really had to deliver.

STARTUP THINKING

We started the journey with the support of an agency – but within a couple of months – it became clear this wasn't a project where agencies could show their strength.

It took months to deliver the strategy because of the complexities of the way Refinitiv works – and I realised you really need to be deeply embedded to understand that and relate it to the new brand identity.

So what we did was to adopt 'startup thinking' and decided to transform the site into a lead-generation powerhouse.

Digital was already driving the majority of leads for the old brand, but our new domain was completely unknown to search engines. In fact, we initially started being outranked by the old website.

Because we had 'no brand', we had to completely re-orient the way the business thinks. That meant shifting from a very brand-heavy website into offering a much more customer-focussed experience, optimised for generic terms.

What worked in our favour was that the older company had a lot of product awareness and loyalty. These products, such as World Check and Eikon, continued to generate traffic and links. So, even though we were invisible to search engines, these products were still being searched for. For that reason, we initially concentrated on quickly regaining this traffic and those links.

PUTTING IN THE WORK

First, I audited all Refinitiv-owned legacy websites and domains, and made a list of mentions and links to all of our brands.

For months on end, my focus was to translate all of our hundreds, if not thousands, of products into more 'human' language, that would, in-turn, translate into search equity.

The language we have to use is not just SEO keywords. It's about being able to explain the product very clearly and knowledgeably.

That's why agencies might have struggled here. We're the ones best placed to understand our product, a fact that became evident the deeper I got into the whole question of what a product was for Refinitiv and our customers.

Next, I conducted a comprehensive gap analysis to see where we were losing key generic terms, as well as looking at the gap compared to our competitors.

There was also a lot of basic site re-architecting to help achieve the mission. We had dozens of legacy websites that we needed to consolidate into one, united digital ecosystem.

We also had to work hard to transform this new site, refinitiv.com, into an authoritative and powerful website, through generating strong links to other reputable sites.

Then we needed to spark significant growth in organic rankings traffic, on a global basis, that converted into significant growth in the amount of leads – and ultimately revenue.

Some of the ways we did this included restructuring the site to target non-brand keywords that were more focused around customer use cases, putting up wholly new pages targeting generic keywords, like 'Brexit's impact on financial markets', and optimising for generic terms like 'market data' and 'M&A data'.

In tactical terms, I had to make some key decisions very early on to make this achievable. Although we operate in more than 190 countries, I decided to focus our local efforts on an initial four high-performing languages, using hreflang for targeting.

I moved to support our data with a lot of new, linkable content such as videos, podcasts and special reports, all hosted on refinitiv.com.

I also set up a rule in our site auditing tool, Crownpeak, to highlight any Thomson Reuters mentions, or links that needed to be updated.

GETTING THE ORGANISATION'S ATTENTION

Educating the rest of the business was no trivial task. A key persuader here was framing the conversation in a way that got people's attention.

If I had just told them 'we have looked at 900,000 keywords and here's some you can use', that doesn't have much narrative weight.

Instead, we told a story about how there are people looking for this kind of solution, and they're now being captured by the competition. 'We're going to lose them to people like Bloomberg because it's better explaining what it provides. Right now, we're way over-reliant on brand alone', we said.

It took months, and dozens of calls to hundreds of people, where we would explain the new Refinitiv SEO strategy in a way that resonated with them, so they could see how it applied to them, their business and their core products.

Another advantage of me doing this in-house was that I was essentially writing a new 'internal bible' about what all the new company's content needed to look like. That document needed to become the 'Holy Grail' for everything we do. To help, we created new page templates and components to enable quick and easy production by teams of new, engaging types of content.

We also did a lot of support and SEO education. We do 'state of search' monthly calls, SEO scorecard reports, performance snapshots emails, SEO workshops and other communication initiatives. This was a big pivot in how we communicated.

INCREASING COMPANY VALUE

So, how did we do? Did this new, in-house-driven SEO strategy for this $6 billion startup get traction?

I had hard targets to meet, after all, we'd been tasked with increasing organic page-one rankings by 40 percent, driving 30 percent growth in organic clicks, growing organic leads by at least 20 percent and generating 20 percent growth in organic-driven revenue.

The results seem to show we did make a difference...

We generated more than 20 million links within a year, establishing refinitiv.com as an authoritative and powerful website that can convincingly compete, and beat, competitors like Factset and IHS Markit.

We also generated over 1,500 leads from our local-language websites, resulting in nearly $1 million in annualised revenue, which busted the targets we had.

Plus, we achieved the desired growth in page-one rankings, with a fivefold increase from January 2019 to December 2019; a 109 percent increase in organic SERP clicks from Q1 to Q4 2019; a record number of leads in Q4; and overall, a 20 percent growth in revenue from digital channels in 2019 versus the year before.

And, I mentioned we were sold on to LSEG, but I didn't mention that they paid $7 billion more than when part of the company was sold to Blackstone, as we'd grown the valuation by 35 percent. That increase was due to the strong company performance and visibility, at least in part led by SEO.

What have I learned that other SEOs could take away as best practice? I think there are five things:

- Major brand changes can be difficult – but a brand transformation can also give you a sense of urgency and focus that can lead to significant achievements.
- Pay close attention to the details – manual, gritty work like updating links may not be pretty, but it is crucial in any successful SEO project.
- Engage stakeholders early and often – this will ensure everyone understands the direction you need to move with SEO and that everyone's goals are aligned.
- Quick wins really help your cause – here, we focused on regaining our top brand terms, which ensured a quick uptick in organic traffic, giving us time to focus on a strategic vision that would target the more challenging and competitive non-brand search terms.
- Keep your eyes on the prize – while we worked to unite the new digital ecosystem, other teams requested our time, but to hit our lead-generation goals, we needed to stay focused. By adopting an '80-20' rule, we managed to support other SEO projects, while driving our core vision forward.

In summary, I would say that in terms of innovation, what stood out here was leveraging our use of our legacy brands, building on our relationship with Thomson Reuters, and taking our market-leading data and turning it into engaging, linkable web content in one, global, united digital ecosystem.

But, in terms of creativity, bringing our SEO work in-house, with a concerted build-out of internal resources and tools to make sure the teams were equipped to succeed, was the standout takeaway for me.

SEO IS SUCH A BIG PART OF THE INFRASTRUCTURE OF AN ORGANISATION – YOU HAVE TO THINK LIKE AN OCTOPUS

LIMOR BARENHOLTZ

SEO DIRECTOR, SIMILARWEB

Limor says that she lives and breathes technical SEO, after spending more than a decade-and-a-half working in a variety of organic and paid online-marketing roles.

Limor's career highlights include spending six years at a major international agency, and eight years working as an in-house SEO.

Most recently – and during Lockdown – she's taken on the challenge of running SEO in-house at Similarweb, where she's focussed on enabling growth.

I found myself looking for a new opportunity last spring when my agency was one of many that needed to manage its budget and reduce headcount.

I wasn't too disappointed for too long, because I saw that Similarweb was looking for someone to set up SEO capabilities, and it's a top brand.

Similarweb is a competitive intelligence tool. We have traffic data on many, many websites, and we can tell you where they get their traffic, what keywords they use, what ads they run, what creatives, and so on. Many digital marketing agencies rely on Similarweb as a research tool.

It's a fantastic environment to be a part of, and I am part of the demand-generation team, working under marketing.

After six years at an agency, it's actually quite heartwarming to be part of something. You're not just recommending things from the outside.

Obviously, you do care about your client's website when you're working at an agency, but you're still an outsider bugging the client to do this, or that. Going back in-house means I am part of something again – and I love it.

BECOMING THE SEO OCTOPUS

That said, the website is a monster. It has millions of pages because we have a page analysis for nearly every website in the world. Then, we have lots of apps, top lists, our own products and then there's all the content we make ourselves, like the blog.

While there had been an SEO consultant visiting, perhaps twice a year, to keep on top of things, it wasn't enough. They would provide pointers on things like improving site speed, but there was no overall picture of the site's architecture.

When you have a tool like ours, there are all sorts of stakeholders. You have the analyst team, the data and big data team, the business intelligence (BI) team, and you have business analysts and marketing analysts.

SimilarWeb

Each one of those teams might be working on a different dataset, or software, or be looking at different things – and all of this is relevant for your job as the new SEO. If that sounds like a lot to get on top of, that's because it is.

Other in-house SEOs will be familiar with this situation, I'm sure. And you just have to sit down and start to organise everything, trying to see where everything fits now and where it should actually be.

I had to try to begin managing that, while also starting a technical-SEO-improvement project.

Alongside that, there's also the internal organisational challenge of making all this happen – when you've only just arrived in the role. Nobody knows you yet, you're not into the politics.

Oh, and there's a global pandemic. It's hitting the ground running in the most exciting way possible.

I had to start thinking like an octopus in order to take it all in at a fast pace. I am racing across the seafloor, with all my little tentacles reaching out and grabbing as much information as I can, to learn as much as I can about this amazing new place.

DOING GOOD, OLD-FASHIONED SEO BEST PRACTICE

What has this little octopus done with all the information she's grabbed? I recently conducted a big audit in the first quarter to see what has happened since I started doing my stuff.

The bottom line was that we saw a 100 percent increase in impressions and visits. I can't say exactly which part of the site, but it was a major, major rise. Non-branded traffic was up 97 percent.

How did I accomplish that? It was just good old-fashioned SEO best practice.

I think maybe 80 percent of that first uplift can be attributed to technical issues that were fixed or improved, like Google readability. Google just wasn't even getting to some of our pages. And our index pages also rose significantly, thanks to those fixes, so now we're ranked for more keywords and we're naturally getting more traffic.

It's very gratifying to see rises both in traffic and ranking, and I am happy to say that it was internal linking that I attribute much of my first wave of in-house SEO success to.

It's just grunt work, not sophisticated software. I just attacked the most glaring site-wide fixes, because I knew they would have the biggest impact. It meant working my way methodically through the code, seeing where the market is and if Google was reading the entire page. Even noticing little things like a page with four H1s – why?

My advice is, when you're approaching a new website for the first time, try to think what the most efficient or fastest way will be to optimise it.

Start with site-wide technical things that you can quickly find, because they will give you (and your sponsors in the business) a great early boost.

This applies just as much to content that people might tell you has already been optimised, by the way. If you optimise the title and you're still taking eight seconds to load, something's clearly not right.

Of course, a big part of the reason you need to talk to everyone when you get in-house is to understand what kind of systems and interfaces we work with.

DOING THE HARD WORK OF COMMUNICATION

So, my sole focus has definitely not just been technical SEO. I know we talk about it a lot within in-house SEO best practice, but communication and making good relationships is also what my 'octopusing' has been about.

Great people skills are very, very important, and even with all my experience, I can tell you I'm not as good at it as I would like to be. So I do the work. I'm having 'virtual coffee' with everyone I can. That includes the brand people, the strategy people, our CEO, the CFO, the CPO, everyone.

I sit down and talk to them about what they're doing and why they're doing it. I'm just learning how I can help them achieve their goals better, asking them to talk to me before they do things that might affect overall SEO. That makes for a busy schedule for me, the SEO octopus.

'I want to be in the meetings – just write to me and I'll join. If I have nothing to say, I won't say anything. I just want to be part of the process here, because we still don't know how to work together'.

'Send me everything you think might have an effect on the website, let me know about every piece of content you're planning on publishing, and we'll take it from there'.

I did a lot of meetings during those first few months, but they were all very necessary in terms of getting those technical fixes done really fast. I really do encourage you to try and be involved in everything at the start of your new in-house SEO journey, because you still don't know which parts are relevant to you.

You don't know which bit of your colleague's work will affect the website. You don't have to manage and oversee every sprint, but I think you do have to know which are the important ones that might have SEO-related implications.

We have had a good start for SEO at Similarweb. But the work continues. Inside six months, according to the plan, there will be four juniors reporting to me who will each have their own path. They will become experts on the product, on our key verticals, and in parallel I will be concentrating on traffic goals. I will also be continuing my role as SEO ambassador and evangelist for the business, communicating how it can contribute to what we do and other people's goals. I am already having really productive early interactions with the product team, about possible improvements or new tools that could help them.

I'm deadly serious when I say that a good SEO has to have a dialogue with everyone, because SEO is such a big part of the infrastructure of the organisation.

Ultimately, it's what you communicate to the outside world, what you want people to think about us when they search. Being an octopus can be challenging... but so much fun!

HOW TO GET FROM OBSCURITY TO THE FRONT PAGE OF GOOGLE

DIMITRIS DRAKATOS

SEO & ASO LEAD, PEANUT

Formerly at UK fintech unicorn Revolut, since October 2020 Dimitris has been leading all the SEO and ASO work at startup Peanut, an app for connecting like-minded women throughout fertility and motherhood.

A passionate digital marketer and SEO manager with more than eight years of experience across both inbound and digital marketing, Dimitris is convinced every SEO can make a difference.

2020... wow. Quite a year, right?

For me, last year involved moving on from one of the biggest startups in the world to a new London-based opportunity, which I'm taking on while being locked down in Athens.

Despite the challenges, I'm certainly learning new things in this job, because my remit includes not just SEO but App Store Optimisation (ASO).

Think of ASO as taking what you do when you're optimising your presence on search engines and applying that to your presence in the Google Play or App Store.

My work is split about 70/30 between those two priorities.

Peanut is a very different field for me. It's a social network designed for women trying to conceive, pregnant women and mothers.

Women can log on and see people just like them. They can swipe up, say hello, make new connections and friendships. Imagine being a member of a Facebook group where it's only people with very close needs to your own.

This job ticked all the boxes for me, because I was really keen on the mission of helping to support women, and I am always keen to be part of a company with strong potential.

STARTING OUT WITH A BLANK SLATE

No matter how crazy things get in your day job, there are certain facts and truths about being a great SEO for your brand, that remain constant.

Firstly, we have all had (or will have) the experience of starting from zero, with a brand that has no visibility.

Everyone knew Revolut by the end of my time there – and Peanut at the moment has no visibility. I've been here before and I think it's very exciting for an SEO to start from nothing, because it showcases to the business just what SEO can do.

Two years from now, our domain will be the hub for any woman searching for answers around conception and pregnancy.

How will we get there? Through content marketing, search optimisation and organic growth, to help both users and users-to-be, and at the same time, helping the company grow. And SEO is at the centre of this strategy.

Once we have 1,000 fully optimised articles, there will be a direct input to the company through SEO and discovery. There will also be indirect benefits, because we can repurpose this content through social media, newsletters and so on.

All the work being done in terms of Peanut SEO will benefit other Peanut media and channels, and I'll briefly map out our plans here. Hopefully this will give reassurance and inspiration if you're an SEO starting with a blank slate.

From day one in the company, you need to start introducing yourself to the team and the key players. It's important that everyone understands what you are doing.

People might have heard of SEO, but there will certainly be people that haven't, or who have incorrect or outdated assumptions about it. You need to say, 'I do SEO – SEO stands for this – and here's how it can benefit our organisation'.

If an engineer is not aware of your arrival, they may make a change that will hurt your plans, or a person from marketing might delete a page without telling you, giving a nice 404 error that will need a day to fix.

Once everyone has visibility of you and you've started to form effective relationships, it will be very important to put in the time to understand what your organisation is offering.

It's crucial you completely understand its product or services and you get up to speed with all of the personas the brand wants to target. This will be crucial for all your later planning – and ultimate success.

FOCUS ON THE EASIER KEYWORDS TO QUICKLY IMPRESS THE CEO

Only now should you start your keyword research. There are so many agencies where people start building their first plan on keywords with queries that are too ambitious and very unrealistic.

They're probably very targeted to your brand, but at the beginning, you have nothing, so keywords with high visibility don't actually help that much. Focus on low-hanging fruit with keywords that are very close to your needs and where your brand can offer solutions.

This will bring you quick wins, meaning you will be happy, but more importantly your manager or the CEO will also be happy.

All this buys you time to start working on more complex keyword research. This should be based on your understanding of the brand, the product and the niche, but at the same time, does look deeply into your main competitors. By this, I mean looking at sites that are ranking for key terms in your content plan.

Very often, I find that search competitors can be different to your ostensible industry competitors, so don't just focus on industry competitors, but also search competitors.

Next, build themes and topic clusters. Here, look to create clusters by organising your keywords by topic. This will help you increase your authority and credibility for both Google search and internal linking, which is very important for the overall searchability of a page.

Content is next. Once you have successfully clustered your keywords, you will have a plan ready. You may have internal or agency resources to help, but take care to find a good writer you trust, as content is a really important factor.

I let the writer know the form every article should follow – this number of bullets, paragraphs and sub-heads - because I need to make sure that the final draft before we publish is close to what I want. This will save you a lot of time going back and forth.

Then, create an internal SEO checklist for your new colleagues. Since you are responsible for SEO, you will be held accountable for both the good and the bad outcomes. Many of us say that SEO is a long-term investment, and for me a good phrase that describes that for people is that SEO is a marathon, not a sprint.

Work to make them understand that, while the returns can be really good, we have to be consistent and persistent to get the most out of it as a brand, and we have to be patient.

MAKING THE CEO EVEN HAPPIER BY WORKING OUT YOUR 'PAYBACK'

Communicating with the business is very important at this stage. We need to be able to show that, if we write a certain number of keywords, the maximum amount of traffic we might get would be some number of million organic visits per month, for example.

You have to make managers aware that we won't be the top result for this keyword at the outset, so set realistic expectations.

Once these building blocks are in place, I would focus on adding more KPIs around organic traffic and conversions.

After the first year, hopefully, you will have good data, including the conversion rate. You can analyse what is working and what isn't, based on this. If you have covered three or four different topics over this time, but one of them has a very large conversion rate compared to the other three, then you should focus on this topic.

Finally, if you want to be more detailed, more proactive and make your CEO even happier – after the first year of SEO making a contribution – start looking in-depth at the payback and customer-lifetime value.

This means knowing that 'we invested this amount of money, we brought back this number of users or installs or sales with this level of conversion, here's the payback'. Don't forget to include your team's salaries in this calculation.

When you have data that shows the customers that you are bringing have a higher lifetime value compared to other sources like paid, this will make your life as the established SEO that much easier.

My ultimate point here is that you just won't have those numbers at the start. You have to do the work and build slowly but surely. But do the work – and be methodical – and you will get the numbers. And that will also help you get from obscurity to that first page of Google.

DO WE REALLY NEED TO KEEP ON SAYING AGENCY 'VERSUS' IN-HOUSE?

I've never worked in an agency – I have always been an in-house SEO person. However, I have worked with agencies to support my work.

Getting the best out of an agency, or knowing when to use one, depends on the level of your seniority and your skills, and how easy it is for you to do it all yourself.

I've worked on the model I describe here a number of times, in various positions, so it's now easy for me to take it and build it internally, with some support.

If you are at a more junior level, you might need some support from an agency. Then, of course, you need to fully understand the resources you'll need and the resources you'll have.

The main disadvantage for a firm of working only with an agency is that there isn't an expert, in-house to have an overview of the work. Agencies can really contribute and really help, but they should be guided by an in-house SEO owner.

SOME GREAT FREE TOOLS WHEN YOU'VE HAD ENOUGH OF AHREFS, SEMRUSH AND MOZ?

Affordable alternatives (free or freemium) that SEOs can use for keyword research, compared to the all-stars:

1. Bing Webmaster Tools (updated version)
2. Ubersuggest
3. LSIGraph
4. keywordtool.io
5. Google Ads Keyword Planner
6. Google Trends

Good luck!

HOW TO SEO AT A NOT-FOR-PROFIT

CHARLOTTE EDWARDS

SEO & ANALYTICS MANAGER, CHATHAM HOUSE

Charlotte has come a long way since she started working as a temp at the London-based international affairs think tank Chatham House six years ago.

She joined after working as a directory publisher and now is responsible for the organisation's SEO, with the support of digital agency Torchbox.

As well as driving traffic to its research, she reports on SEO statistics to senior staff at a weekly meeting.

One of her favourite stats? Annual sessions on the Chatham House website have increased by more than 50 percent since she started. Here, she tells us a little about how she did that.

Until I joined Chatham House, there was no real awareness of SEO, outside of our digital team. I'd only recently started to become aware of it myself, to be frank...

I started on the team as a temp and was offered the opportunity to stay and learn on the job. I really did have to jump in.

Back then, we were just about to launch a new version of the website – and 2020 was all about updating that again, with a new site launched in October 2020.

The 15,000 pages, and more, on our website largely hold content by academics and researchers, most of them experts in their fields.

I have, perhaps, a different set of targets compared to SEOs working in commercial or even public-sector organisations, because most of our sources of funding are offline. So I've had to find other incentives for our writers, as we don't measure everything gained from SEO in revenue terms.

First, I thought, if I'm going to get experts interested in how their content is performing, I need to know how they're doing with their content now. To build an SEO-friendly culture, I had to begin by showing them why it was in their interest to care about Google.

LEARNING TO BE A NOT-FOR-PROFIT SEO

For the first relaunch, I was mainly doing back-end work – taxonomy classification and data entry. Then I was introduced to Google Analytics. Torchbox agreed to train me up and it all really started from there.

This was in the days before Google Data Studio, so for all 13 of our programmes, every quarter, I was doing individual reports in Excel analysing how each piece of content was performing, in what countries.

This was also in the days when Google still had the Network Domain dimension, so one of my first major projects was to pull six months of data from Google Analytics and use it to create a set of regexes, which then became segments for our priority audience sectors.

It was a lot of hard work. But it meant I could go to my stakeholders and show them how the piece they'd written about Sudan had been read 55 times there, as well as by people from the UK's Ministry of Defence, the Office of the Nigerian President, and so on.

My colleagues really liked that, because in most cases, their financing comes from funding applications, and the people awarding funds want reports on how any content has performed.

Still, one of my favourite parts of the job is when somebody new writes their first piece for the website. I give it a week or two, then I track the stats and send them an email that I copy to their manager, pointing out all the countries where their content has been read and the significant audience members who read it. It always makes them so happy.

BUILDING INTERNAL SEO SUPPORT

When colleagues realised they could come to me and I could give them a lot of useful information to go into their reports, suddenly, it became a question of how else we could work together.

I started dropping in how content they'd created had reached all these countries and ranked highly in Google, because Google liked the keywords they used. Soon, the researchers got the idea that 'if I use these particular words, it will help'. I also built each of our programme teams their own individual Data Studio dashboards, so they could see how their content was doing for themselves.

With the support of Torchbox, my current big project is a new set of dashboards to go with the new site, based firmly on SEO and UX principles, and which are able to tell the programme teams everything they need to know. We're also widening our focus to concentrate on qualitative metrics – how much people engage with our content, what makes them convert and keep coming back – as much as quantitative ones.

Once the experts got the idea that these SEO statistics were interesting, they wanted more of them. And then they realised that organic search was a good thing – and it would benefit them to be working with our content team on SEO.

All of this evangelism has really paid off because now I present to an audience, including senior members of staff, every week – and they ask questions about how we're performing.

GOING PUBLIC

Building this SEO internal visibility has been particularly important because there's been a recent shift in what we want to achieve.

Now, we want to expand the audience for our content beyond our usual constituency to more of the general, global public. We want to get the public interested in our content and to be as inclusive as possible.

In terms of the site relaunch, our biggest concern was all the horror stories we'd heard about with site migrations. For the past two years, I've been keeping a KPI tracker, so I knew that our general benchmarks were things like, how long people stayed on the site, how people got to the site, and so on.

We were expecting numbers to drop after the relaunch, but we worked really hard, got all the redirects sorted and made sure that everything was set up correctly. We definitely didn't do the classic thing of forgetting to remove the 'noindex' tag.

We did see numbers drop at first, but they started recovering again within about six weeks, and now they're better than ever.

Here, we took the opportunity to have a massive clear out, archiving older content and making sure that the only pieces that stayed were still getting lots of views.

I suspect many of us have things we always mean to clear up but never get around to. This was the perfect opportunity. We had a rule that, any content that was over five years old, unless it fitted very specific criteria, would be archived, and that's made a big difference.

We wanted the new website to work well for both users, and search engines, and that's still our main focus.

On the content side, we're working all the time to optimise SEO and user experience for all our pages. On the technical side, we focussed on getting the internal links, Javascript and redirects right pre-launch, now we're maximising speed. My favourite tool for tech audits is Sitebulb Web Crawler – it's versatile and user-friendly.

I've also found some of the Google Sheets add-ons really useful, especially if I'm trying to pull a lot of data at once. My favourite tool for avoiding sampling issues is the Google Analytics Spreadsheet add-on and I combine that with the Google Query visualisation tool to get some really interesting data. I'm also learning Python, which has its challenges, but I think it will be really useful.

If I had to sum up my work as an SEO in a non-profit after six years, I'd say that we've achieved a lot. There are now 10 of us on the Digital Transformation team, and everyone's taking an interest in SEO and data – it's a wonderful team to be part of.

We also have invaluable help with SEO, analytics and digital marketing from digital agency Torchbox. There's always a challenge and always something new to learn or achieve.

And that's why I love my job.

HOW TO BE REALLY EFFECTIVE IN-HOUSE AS A NON-PROFIT SEO

An important lesson that I learned early on in my career is, when people ask questions, it's never just about you answering their question – it's about working out what they actually want.

Someone might come to me and say they need to know how many hits we had on a page. And I need to check if they really mean 'hits', or if they mean interesting numbers. Also – who is really asking for the numbers? Because, if it's a funder, they might have specific criteria for the numbers they need to see.

I'm careful to always take this step because I want to ensure the information someone gets from me is really what they need.

So if you ask, 'who watched something', do you actually want that filtered for a particular kind of audience, in a particular country? More often than not, it turns out they want specific visitors from specific governments, for example. As I am usually time-constrained, if I know what they really need, I can go straight there and say, 'I think you'll find this helpful'.

My other advice is to be as accurate as you can, but warn the stakeholder if you can't be. Say 'I can give you the accurate figures in two hours, or you can have an estimation now'. I think this sort of conversation builds trust.

Finally, be sensitive to your audience. There's an enormous difference between what I would provide for a meeting of the 'top team' versus the SEO detail I would give my direct boss.

If I'm doing something for Chatham House's director, I don't assume they've heard of Google Analytics, and I wouldn't expect them to, because it's not their priority. The senior executive team needs something high-level and intuitive, whereas my line manager will want something a bit more granular, so we can sit there and talk through it.

WHY SEOS ARE INDISPENSABLE – AND HOW THEY CAN SHOW IT

BEN JOHNSON

FREELANCE

Ben Johnson was introduced to SEO as part of Sky's digital marketing team in the late noughties and has since worked with major brands including Rightmove and Network Rail.

Today he is working as a freelance SEO, has taught himself programming on the side and is an enthusiast about 'all things digital marketing'.

He is also the founder of SiteKite.io, an automated SEO-testing tool.

Ben is a returning contributor to this book and this year he explains how to show that you're indispensable as an SEO.

When you work in SEO, not all companies get what you do. Developers think you're marketing and marketing thinks you're tech. Everyone else just thinks you're a practitioner of the dark arts. It's like the embodiment of those Venn diagrams, where SEO is that little circle that falls between two different departments.

So – if SEO is the black sheep of the marketing family – what can you do as an in-house SEO to get recognition and value for work that few really understand?

HELP MAKE YOUR COLLEAGUES' VISION A REALITY

The most important thing to remember is that SEO is a cross-discipline skillset: you've laid the foundations with technical SEO, you're creating great content, you're doing off-page activities, or outsourcing it to a third-party and managing that relationship.

You're always working with other marketing channels too. You help the PR team to build links, and encourage the social team to share your great SEO content far and wide. It's all got to work like one well-oiled machine if the project is going to be successful.

One thing a lot of marketing teams don't have is technical expertise. Often, as an SEO, I will hijack the blog and post content that I know I need to write. But when other internal stakeholders decide they want to create blog content, one of the ways I look to add value is being a point of contact to help them. They might want to embed an infographic, or add terms and conditions to a page in a drop-down or smaller font. As an SEO, you know HTML, CSS and probably a bit of JavaScript, so you can help them make their vision a reality.

SEOs also spend a lot of time in Google Tag Manager. There's a ton of stuff you can do with this, but let's imagine the marketing team wants to change something on the website very quickly, that isn't accessible via the Content Management System, perhaps a 'hero image' or a colour change on a 'call to action'.

Quite often the development team can't help immediately, but one of the things I can do as an SEO is to implement it through Google Tag Manager using Javascript. Obviously, I'm always careful to let the developers know I'm only doing it as a stop-gap solution until they can implement something more permanent.

This sort of 'hero work' helps you become more embedded in the marketing team. You're the SEO person who is helping out, going beyond your remit, and you're likely the only person with the technical ability to do that. It's by making yourself a subject-matter expert that you can really become indispensable to the wider marketing team.

This also opens up a dialogue with the development team, and you might end up being a conduit between the marketing and development teams as a result. I'm a big advocate of automated SEO testing. This is about making sure the site is running quickly, that important elements aren't broken, and making sure all our pages are working as intended. If you have an in-house QA team, or even a developer who is a stickler for perfection, then this can be a great way to build value (and relationships) outside of just marketing.

BECOME 'ONE' WITH THE LEAN, MEAN, MARKETING MACHINE

Another important set of stakeholders to befriend are the in-house Pay Per Click (PPC) team. For one of my long-term freelance clients, I'm working with that team to optimise one of our key landing pages to create a better user experience. This is great for me as an SEO, because a better user experience means better signals being sent to Google about the page quality, and hopefully it will help with 'stickiness'.

At the same time, though, from a PPC perspective, any improvements you can make to UX will improve the overall 'quality score' of that page. This means conversion rates will be better, so the CPCs are also going to be lower. It's a win-win situation.

Many SEOs don't link up with PPC teams to get 'double buy-in' – but here's why it's important – getting double buy-in means that senior managers are more likely to sign-off on improvement projects because both teams are pitching together.

I've also always worked very closely with PR teams. As an SEO, I can help with understanding what sort of PR initiatives might resonate best with certain target audiences, and help to input ideas into PR roadmaps. A lot of those ideas will be related to data gathering and questionnaires. They're content marketing, effectively.

What I'll do is work with the PR team to create landing pages that maximise the likelihood that we'll get backlinks from press releases, and often I use crawlers to help with data collection too (looking at you, custom extraction).

When it's all ready to go, I will help with constructing the press release and work closely with them on the outreach. I might do some link-building, or reach out to lower-level blogs while they're doing the outreach to top-tier publications. Having this kind of synergy with PR can really add value to the PR function, but it also adds value to SEO.

The SEO can also help out the social media team by letting them know about new and exciting SEO content you're creating. I create a lot of content for one of my clients and at the end of each week, I send the social media team a summary. That helps them because they have a collection of new content to share, which makes their lives easier.

SHOW THE CMO AND CEO WHAT YOU KNOW

Here's a really important tip – SEOs can and should be using the wealth of SEO tools we have at our disposal to give CMOs and CEOs greater insights about competitors. I do this a lot when I come in and do an SEO audit for new clients.

Our SEO tools allow us to gauge (however crudely) how much competitors are spending on PPC, or what keywords they are bidding. You can use Semrush to pull estimates of where the opposition's Google spend is going, whether they're paying for display ads, all the way down to what their latest set of display creatives look like.

I can also expand this service with non-SEO tools like Google Keyword Planner. This lets me tell a CMO about how branded searches for their competitors are going. 'Is their increased PPC spend also driving an increase in branded searches? What about those display ads - do they seem to be driving higher brand awareness?'. All of these insights are invaluable to the business.

Ultimately, you can add value over and above SEO just by taking more of an active interest in what matters to your peers. If you take a second to start thinking holistically about how your unique skills can help other areas of marketing, it will help your SEO work. It will also help the company. And it means you won't end up being put in the corner because people don't know what you do.

TECH TIP CORE WEB VITALS

Google has been using Site Speed as a small part of its ranking algorithm, primarily on mobile, for the last few years. In 2021, it's going to be expanding it to include something called 'Core Web Vitals'. It's Site Speed on steroids. Site Speed 2.0.

What's different this time is that Core Web Vitals are not just about how quickly a page loads, but also consider other visual elements and user experiences related to page load.

One key one is 'Cumulative Layout Shift', a ridiculous name for a great concept. This covers how much a website page moves around even after the user thinks it has fully loaded. For example, have you ever tried to click on a button the second before a 'helpful' tooltip appears and budges the button down a bit? It's annoying - and this is why Google wants us to think more about web design through a user experience lens.

Also included is something called 'First Input Delay', which relates to how long it takes for user interactions to be noticed by the browser, and 'Largest Contentful Paint', which measures the time it takes for the largest piece of content to be shown on the screen.

I'm an advocate of Core Web Vitals and believe that Google's focus on them will drive tangible and wide-reaching improvements to user experience on the web. However, as with many of these ideologically-driven algorithm updates, it almost certainly won't have any meaningful impact on rankings. Slow sites will still rank highly when they have great content, and fast sites will still rank poorly when they don't have any authority behind them.

This doesn't mean SEOs shouldn't be interested in this area, or indeed, driving these changes, but it's more interesting to look at this from a user-experience perspective.

It's also a good reminder that ultimately Google is moving to a place where it wants every user experience to be fantastic, in support of its own mission statement, "to organise the world's information and make it universally accessible and useful".

IT'S THE MICRO-INTERACTIONS YOU HAVE EVERY DAY THAT MAKE THE REAL DIFFERENCE TO YOUR SEO CREDIBILITY

AMANDA KING

SEO MANAGER, OPTUS

Sydney-based Amanda describes herself as a book and travel nerd that just happened to get into 'solving puzzles' as an SEO.

Her career started in the days when SEO was a matter of 'exact match keyword stuffing', but these days, Amanda approaches digital marketing with a business-focused perspective.

Her current role is helping Australian telco giant Optus with a range of SEO and project-management skills.

At time of interview Amanda was SEO Specialist at Optus

Whatever SEO role I've had, I have always gone in with the desire to make an impact.

In many ways, Optus is the challenger brand in the Australian market, and my mission is to help it make a bigger impact on as wide an audience as possible.

In our organisation, SEO reports to marketing, but we sit with the sales 'tribe', because that team manages the sales pages of the website, so it makes sense to be where we can be most effective and useful.

I have a team of about eight people in SEO, with a variety of skills and specialisms, from content to personalisation.

At Optus, SEO is really about improving the bottom line. That's always going to be our end goal. Most organisations are revenue-driven, after all.

But, our wider mission and vision is around constantly improving the customer experience, because Optus aims to be Australia's most loved everyday brand. That means we need to offer a smooth, fast and clear experience.

Sometimes, that might mean doing technical work to improve site speed, other times, it might be doing A/B testing of content.

But it always comes back to improving the customer experience.

A YEAR OF EFFORT AND EDUCATION

We recently completed a project that made Optus the only telco on the first page of Google for the latest iPhone launch.

Getting there took a year of coordinated effort and education with our developer teams and designers around website performance, JS impacts and file size.

And it illustrates just how well we've integrated SEO into what we're trying to achieve as a business.

It's no exaggeration to say this took a year – the conversation started right after the launch of the iPhone 11 in September 2019.

I had joined Optus in-house at the end of June and by mid-July we were already starting to prepare for the next iPhone.

The problem at this point was that I was 'the new SEO girl'. Because nobody knew who I was, I couldn't really tell people that we needed to change the way things were written because it's affecting our visibility, or that we needed to write code in a different way.

We performed very well among the telecom providers for the iPhone 11 launch, but I knew it could have been a lot better.

So, from that moment on, I started talking to all of our different teams and learning more about how our website was built, because I knew that for any iPhone launch, it's always a high-traffic point.

To maximise our opportunity with any new iPhone, we always split those pages from the rest of our website.

We sit it on a different server, and write it in a completely different library, so that if those pages go down due to traffic, it doesn't affect the rest of our website.

However, I didn't know the script it was written in, so before I did anything else, I sat down and started learning about Angular...

I was also chipping away in the background by keeping up a conversation with development about why the pages were built this way. Over time, I was able to say that, if we did it another way, Google would be able to see this great information sooner.

I did the same thing with our designers. I started talking to them about how I could see we have all these image files that were PNGs, but perhaps we could use JPEGs instead. I needed to know how comfortable they would be with me compressing those files, before they would start worrying about image quality.

I'd also been talking to one of our accessibility experts to learn more about alt attributes. I didn't always look at them through the lens of pure accessibility, but I've started handling them a lot differently this year.

Now I'm trying to understand the nuances, like when you need to include a full stop in an alt attribute, because this actually pauses the screen reader, and so gives the person the breathing space to know this is the end of that statement. Little things like that can be really important.

TURNING STRANGERS INTO COLLABORATORS

Really, it was about having a lot of open conversations with all the people who would be my collaborators on the upcoming iPhone page. I had to be sensitive, because it's their work as well – I don't want to come in and dictate – I wanted to find a middle ground that would work for everyone.

These conversations and pre-work for the upcoming iPhone went on for months and months – and it all culminated in the most recent set of iPhone launches in late 2020.

By then, my designers knew, without asking, what my file size limits were and came to me directly saying, 'this file is going to be a bit bigger – but I'm not really comfortable compressing it. Is that okay?'.

The most important part of my preparation for the iPhone 12 launch at Optus was working very closely with the developers and our Angular library. We wanted to be able to get a page up ready for the announcement that would match the product URL, so the URLs remained consistent and persistent. That meant our presence in Google never really dipped during that critical 48-hour period between announcement and pre-order.

Having a consistent URL where Google could see our content was critical. I wouldn't have been able to achieve that if it hadn't been for the time taken with the developers to understand the Angular build, and to have built a common mindset about what we wanted.

Starting early also meant we would have time to make changes to the Angular set-up if we needed to.

SPEAK THEIR LANGUAGE AND DON'T BE AFRAID TO ASK QUESTIONS

I don't have any kind of dollar value on what all of this preparation did for us when the iPhone 12 launched in Australia. But what I can tell you is that we had 33 percent higher visibility during pre-order for the iPhone 12, versus the iPhone 11. We also saw a similar increase in organic traffic year-on-year.

Perhaps we shouldn't be surprised when SEO makes this sort of contribution to the business – but I think it can come as a surprise in big companies.

Big ships can be hard to get to shift course and I think my co-workers were very used to looking at things from one, familiar angle. I was able to come in and bring a different perspective. But, unless it's something you've been doing consistently in your organisation for a long time, SEO is still a very ambiguous thing, and everyone has their own understanding of it.

A lot of what I have done with Optus has been a combination of communication and building relationships.

That's what I always try to do – putting the benefits of SEO into the language that someone else speaks. If I am speaking to a lot of engineers, or speaking to a lot of front-end developers, I talk about page performance and code and server lag, because I know that performance is a big priority for this community.

For our legal teams I'll talk more about accessibility and compliance. For marketing, I'll talk about sales, revenue impacts and conversion rates. For me, the success of in-house SEO comes down to being able to speak in the other person's language.

I would also stress the importance of acknowledging that you don't know everything in their field of expertise. I would never say I know everything about JavaScript SEO. Instead, I am saying, we need to do this thing because it would help us all, but it's very much a collaborative effort.

Does that sound like a lot of languages to learn? I hope not. For me, the best place to start is always being humble and unafraid to ask questions. If I was working on a website that was in a JS library that I didn't understand, I would find the person who built that page and just ask them questions.

I am also really transparent about the fact that I see all this from an SEO perspective and that if we did things this way, we could really improve our visibility.

More often than not, the subject-matter experts will know the solution to what you're trying to do. But it may not be the first thing they came up with, because they're not used to speaking SEO language, either.

HOW WE MADE OUR WEBSITE BETTER FOR USERS – WITHOUT STARTING FROM SCRATCH – AND HOW YOU CAN TOO

VIOLETTE MOUSSAVI

SEO & DIGITAL MARKETING MANAGER, GREENDROPSHIP

After six years in a range of SEO roles, including in-house and agency positions, Violette is currently running the marketing department for GreenDropShip.com from its Los Angeles office. The US-based company distributes organic and natural groceries, as well as body-care and wellness products, to ecommerce retailers. Violette also works as an SEO Consultant, implementing organic-growth initiatives for emerging brands that want to improve search visibility.

I prefer to work in-house as an SEO because I think you can be more deeply involved. I've worked in both agency and in-house roles, but I always enjoy being in-house more, because I know I'll have more freedom to implement my preferred strategy.

I don't need to convince clients on the importance of making this change, or wait for them to implement my recommendations.

I am doing just that in my role at GreenDropShip. We supply organic and natural products to Shopify, WooCommerce and Amazon merchants, and manage the order fulfillment. My current focus is definitely content SEO, because our main source of traffic is organic, and my mission is to build brand visibility in search engines.

When I joined the company, I was the first person to lead the SEO and marketing efforts. GreenDropShip had only been in operation for two years and, for this relatively new B2B brand, gaining more visibility in SERPs was necessary to acquire more customers.

Essentially, I needed to create an SEO content strategy that would increase rankings and traffic, and in turn, drive conversions and revenue.

Our founder had some knowledge of SEO and had previously worked with content writers to maintain our blog. However, I still needed to start from scratch when I took over, which meant assembling a writing team and training them on SEO best practice.

We started producing a lot of content on the blog, under pressure to rank for as many targeted keywords as possible. But after some time, I realised that I needed to take a different approach, because we were publishing new content that would cover the same topic as our older articles.

One issue with this was that overlapping posts would be seen as duplicate content in the eyes of search engines. But it also didn't provide any more value to our users.

As a result, I decided to change our content strategy to improve our organic performance, and at the beginning of 2020, I built a new plan. Instead of creating new articles, I decided to repurpose and consolidate the existing content. I had a hunch that it could help improve their rankings and move them up to page one.

WHAT TO CONSIDER BEFORE REPURPOSING

I established the following process before repurposing the content:

Step 1 – identify blog posts with overlapping content.

Step 2 – review their rankings and organic performance.

Step 3 – decide which URL to keep, to redirect or to unpublish.

After this, the most important part was working with the content writers to repurpose the blogs posts, which I'll explain more about.

But first, I want to explain more about how you focus on a specific search query and identify all pages with overlapping content. A simple way to find duplicate or similar pages is to use the Google search operator site:domain.com 'keyword'. This will show you how many pages on your website have this keyword in the metadata or URL.

After identifying duplicate pages, I analysed the rankings for each one of these URLs, but also looked at their organic performance and user engagement metrics, such as bounce rate.

If we had a blog post that was ranking, but had a high bounce rate, it was an opportunity for us to revisit that post because our goal was to provide content that would help users convert.

The next steps, which are not always that obvious, are to decide which URL to choose and which posts to consolidate. Sometimes, it is easy as you have one URL that is ranking and others that don't rank. But in other cases, we had multiple URLs ranking for the same keyword. The two scenarios below summarise what was going on.

Scenario 1 – multiple pages ranking for the same keyword:

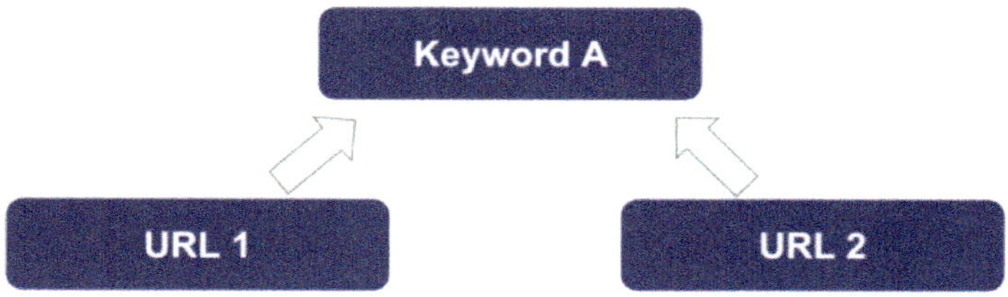

'URL 1' is ranking for 'keyword A'

'URL 2' is also ranking for 'keyword A'

Solution – merge content to keep only one URL and implement a 301 redirect.

When multiple URLs rank for the same keyword, it means that they are effectively competing for the same search intent. Merging them into one post would help improve its rank, instead of sending a confusing signal to search engines.

On a case-by-case basis, we had to decide if we wanted to consolidate 'URL 1' and 'URL 2', but I first needed to determine which one it made more sense to keep.

If 'URL 1' was more meaningful or had a higher-quality piece of content that better satisfied the searcher's intent, that was the URL that we had to keep. That meant all we had to do was merge the content of both posts to add more value to the article.

Finally, we had to redirect 'URL 2' to 'URL 1' so as to pass the link equity to the main piece of content. Here's an example of a blog post that gained an immediate increase in traffic after we repurposed the content:

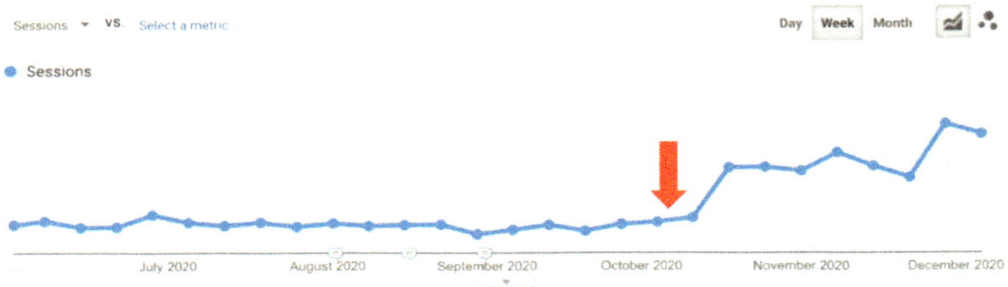

Scenario 2 – many articles targeted the same keyword but not all of them ranked:

Solution – remove content that does not rank and repurpose the best pieces of content.

When different pages targeted the same query but they didn't rank, it didn't make sense to keep all of them. The obvious solution here has to be to remove content that does not rank or provide any value.

The rubric we adopted was that the page that ranked higher was the most relevant page to keep, other pages should be unpublished, as users weren't finding them anyway.

Such a move also stopped us giving split ranking signals to Google and prevented search engines from crawling multiple pages on our site targeting the same keyword.

As a final step, we updated the content of the ranking post to add more value, working to make it more engaging and helpful for the users.

HOW TO REPURPOSE CONTENT WITH THE USER IN MIND

To repurpose the content, while providing the best experience for users, we adopted the following tactics:

- Identify the search intent.
- Review competitors' pages that rank for the same query.
- Research how to add value to the post.
- Optimise the outline and start writing the post.

To improve the quality of the content, we had to make sure the page satisfied the search intent for the query we wanted to rank for. Always ask yourself what the user expects to read after performing that search. You can also identify the search intent by doing a Google search, using your keywords. You'll see what type of results you get, whether it is an informative blog post, a product-focused page, a list page, comparison, and so on.

If you want to rank for 'how to start an online store', users would expect to find in any search result things like the type of ecommerce platform they could use, how to set up their store, what products they might sell and how to promote their store to make sales.

Your outline should include all the sections listed above, to make sure you provide the information that helps answer that query.

After determining the search intent, I reviewed the competitors' content that was ranking for that query on page 1 to find out how to make ours even more unique. In my industry, some of our core topics describing our services already get a lot of coverage on other (competitor) websites. This doesn't mean we shouldn't target those queries, but it does mean we have to differentiate our content if we want to rank for the same search query.

As a result, I created another rule for our team. Before creating any new blog posts, we need to analyse the SERPs to see what pages already rank for that term. The best way to outrank competitors, after all, is to carefully review their content and find out how to provide more value to users.

You will be surprised how often you can run into a competitor page that is ranking but doesn't provide the best experience for users. And as any good in-house SEO will know, there are proven ways to add value. You could provide additional information on the topic, add your own research with more data, interview experts, or make your piece easier to read.

In my experience, especially in agencies, most managers who work with content writers just provide a keyword and a topic. But getting this right takes a lot more than that. I work closely with content writers to structure the page and come up with an optimised outline.

Every blog post has to have a clear outline with meaningful heading tags (H1, H2, H3) enabling the reader to understand the content just by looking at the headings. After all, most users don't take the time to read everything.

Adding the right internal links and structuring the content properly for users does, in turn, make the page more meaningful to search engines, which results in higher rankings. The writers should also have the proper SEO guidance to understand how to make their content rank and perform better.

DID ALL OF THIS HARD WORK PAY OFF?

In early 2020, we implemented our new content strategy. I am glad to say that the needle, as they say, has definitely moved for GreenDropship. We've seen a significant increase in both keyword rankings and organic traffic.

Our website organic traffic is now up over 200 percent year-on-year (the arrow indicates when changes were inaugurated):

Organic traffic in 2020 vs 2019:

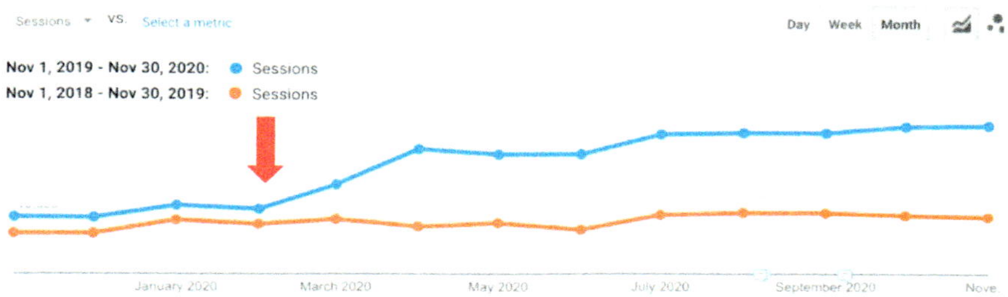

Source: Google Analytics

Finally, I always encourage SEOs to keep track of any changes that they implement. If you test a tactic and it works, easily knowing what you did will help get quicker results next time.

Developing your organic visibility involves more than SEO and content optimisation. Google's algorithm updates tend to improve user experience, so this is the direction SEOs should also keep going in. You can provide the best content, but if users don't trust your website and you don't come across as an expert on the topic, they won't convert.

That's why focusing on developing your overall user experience, and building your brand, is the way to go. Establish yourself as an authority in your industry, implement different marketing strategies to get brand mentions and don't just focus on how to optimise the website for keywords.

SEO is now about making sure you have a strong brand – that attracts users – who convert.

That's where I believe SEO will be going. I wonder what you think?

WHY YOU SHOULD MAKE SEO-DEV RELATIONSHIPS A CONSTANT PRIORITY – AND THREE WAYS TO DO IT

ORIT MUTZNIK

HEAD OF SEO, SILKFRED

Working as an in-house SEO for more than a decade means Orit Mutznik has built up an impressive CV – but it's her language skills, deployed across a range of marketing fields, that she thinks help her get things done as an SEO.

She's a linguistics graduate, and is fluent in English, Hebrew and Spanish, enabling her to take international leadership roles, lastly at investment platform eToro.

Last year, alongside making Search Engine Journal's list of top SEO experts, she told us how she achieved her relocation dream. Now, she's living it, having recently moved to London to become Head of SEO at independent-fashion ecommerce platform SilkFred – and she still believes 'speaking other people's language' is key.

If you make clothes and don't quite know where to start in the online world, you can come to SilkFred and we will market them for you.

I've been in this role for over two challenging years now, establishing SEO from scratch. There was no proper SEO effort or marketing channel in the business prior to me joining. There were some very talented developers who knew more than a thing or two and the rare SEO-agency consultation, nothing else.

Part of my role as Head of SEO is to make our website more accessible to Google, but I also need to help these small-, or even micro-, brands be more discoverable. I share as much as I can with our partners about what they need to do for people to find their products more easily.

But the most important thing is the technical side, by a landslide, so that's where I focus the vast majority of my efforts, and so making excellent SEO-dev relationships is a constant priority.

Just before I came on board, I was asked to conduct a full audit to spot high-level SEO opportunities, and out of that process I built two roadmaps: a high-level one for senior brand stakeholders, complemented by a more detailed, tech-SEO roadmap. That latter piece of work became my first step in building a good relationship with the development team.

We started well when I realised the person sitting in front of me had (unknowingly) led all previous SEO efforts in the business. Essentially that was just by taking search-engine visibility into account in their technical work, as far as they knew it was relevant. In addition, some parts of my new SEO plan required aspects of site caching and speed that had been championed independently of SEO. So that meant I got myself an internal champion before I even started drawing salary.

While some SEOs do the bare minimum on this front and still get their way eventually, building successful stakeholder relationships, especially with the developers, makes the job much easier. Why doesn't this happen more? A lot of SEOs tell me they don't see the value of building relationships. They think they can get stuff done without that side of things. But if you build good, strong relationships with colleagues, you can do better work, faster.

That is definitely how it's been for me. It's been much easier for me to request things and get them done quickly, which is always one of the perennial challenges in SEO.

And, for me, successful Dev-SEO-business relationships are built on three critical principles:

1. AGILITY AND FLEXIBILITY

The first thing you need to understand about a growing startup, especially when it's trying to set up a new marketing channel, is that things happen fast. Priorities change quickly, so you have to be ready to fight for what you need.

It also means that access to budget and resources can be variable; sometimes you're at the top of the priority list and sometimes you're not. As much as it is your job to champion SEO and be relentless about that, accepting that things can't always go your way, and being okay with waiting, will help you keep calmer and a lot saner (while you wait for the right time to push).

2. EDUCATION

Whether you're the first SEO in the business or joining an existing effort, stakeholder education is critical. When I joined SilkFred, I created three different versions of 'An Intro to SEO' slides and switched the deck according to which team I was presenting to. It's important to make these sessions interesting, engaging, clear, simple and relatable.

A good foundation goes a long way towards getting better deliverables, faster, from your new colleagues, because you've saved yourself a lot of time explaining the value of what you do again and again. It also means the people working with you are more likely to be onboard with what you want SEO to do for them.

When you're not the first SEO, education is still needed. It just needs to be even smarter and more in-tune with previous educational efforts. Talking to all the main stakeholders will give you a feel of their level of understanding of the value of SEO, and how engaged they are, so you can tailor your interactions with them appropriately.

3. SIMPLICITY AND TRANSPARENCY

The most common question I am asked is about 'effort versus impact'. In SMEs, your ROI, or how to prioritise SEO work within the business, is often measured by the amount of development time that's required for a specific task. So, to give my colleagues a useful business answer, I use the Impact-Effort Matrix developed by Patrick Stox of Ahrefs.

In this methodology, every task is assigned an effort level that is previously agreed with the developers, based on the task taking from hours, to days or weeks. The task is then assigned a value (low, medium or high) and an impact (also low, medium or high) and it's the responsibility of the SEO to prove those values. For example you might say that by getting 'x' done, we'll be able to build a landing page for a search term that is searched by 300,000 people per month in our target country.

This tool means I can easily prioritise low-effort, high-impact outcomes, which have the best chance of happening quickly, despite the scarcity of resources.

High-effort, high-impact tasks will probably become full-on roadmap projects that I will need to build a more solid case for. An example of this would be providing the technical infrastructure to meet Core Web Vitals ahead of the May 2020 Google Page Experience Update. I always plan for this to take more time, but this is better than not happening at all, due to not having a proper 'voice' among stakeholders.

The key is mostly simplicity in the breakdown of the task, accompanied by transparency on the effort vs impact equation.

Applying these principles got me the resource I needed to implement that technical SEO roadmap that I had in my pocket when I arrived at SilkFred. But, of course, the roadmap got bigger over time, as I became more familiar with the technical setup of the business and teams, allowing us to triple our SEO visibility.

GETTING THE REST OF THE BUSINESS ON BOARD

Getting business stakeholders' buy-in to SEO's potential really matters, too. Business stakeholders will challenge you – and you have to be able to give them the kind of commercial answers they need.

You need to do your homework and get the data you need to back up your claims, come back with your requirements, reflect that confidence in your knowledge and be ready to answer questions.

SEO professionals do not invest enough time in these internal politics and 'soft skills', which is a shame, because it's something that is going to make your life so much easier. I think it's so important to talk about this, as you may be surprised to know how much good 'people skills' can help you. That little bit of bridge building actually made my onboarding so much easier and accelerated my chance to contribute. And it's been truly rewarding as an SEO to work on building a relationship with my development team.

Overall, you're going to be much more effective if you can do this, and the results you bring to the organisation will be much more impactful. So, step out of SEO for a moment, and open your mind to looking at what other teams are doing. You can then initiate conversations to better understand their roles – and find the best way to drive your SEO agenda.

WHY A GROWTH MINDSET IS THE SEO'S BEST TOOL

MORDY OBERSTEIN

HEAD OF COMMUNICATIONS, SEMRUSH

Israel-based SEO veteran Mordy describes himself as an SEO educator.

That's perhaps not surprising, as he is a qualified teacher, but these days, his role is to evangelise the WIX platform as its official SEO liaison.

Mordy has learned a great deal about SEO by working in many parts of the sector, including time spent with SEO tool vendor Rank Ranger.

At time of interview Mordy was SEO Community Liaison at Wix

We spend a lot of time in SEO agonising about what Google just did, or is about to do, or what its real intentions are – and in some respects – SEO is hard because Google is a 'great mystery'.

So it's not hard to see why we SEOs like concrete things and clear rules. Because we can't know what Google is doing, so it's comforting falling back on tangible things.

But I can't really understand this obsession, because to me, it's very clear what Google is asking us to do. Perhaps that can only become clear for all SEOs if we change our focus – to adopt what I call a 'growth mindset'...

UNDERSTANDING THE LIMITS OF SEO DATA

One problem here is that sticking to such technical rules can give you a false sense of achievement.

The same goes for SEO data. It's easy to over-rely on it. That might surprise you coming from someone who worked at Rank Ranger – and loved it.

But ranking is a false metric, and most SEO data in general is problematic, because we look at data without mapping it onto the real world. You can't understand the actual story the data tells until you understand its confines.

When you do a study at grad school, the first thing you do is put in qualifiers. What are the limitations of the study?

We never do that when we look at SEO data. We need to think about what this data can tell us. How can I use it? Where do we go next? And, what is beyond the scope of the data? Because data is never the end goal. It only helps us know what questions to ask – and what path to follow.

RANKING WITHOUT CONTEXT

Not to beat up on rank tracking, but we are often too reliant on that, too.

Let's say you're ranking number one for best hotel in New York City during Covid. That's fantastic, but no-one's going to hotels right now and no one's searching for that. So, who cares?

You might say that traffic matters, but if nobody is buying the product, it's irrelevant. Traffic without conversions is pointless. If you get hung up on one aspect of it, you're not helping your site.

You need to think about SEO as the sum of all its parts. That means taking SEO from a more holistic point of view including the site's identity, authority and overall brand perception.

It requires us to think of a site from an ever-active growth mindset.

It's very striking that when Google puts out a statement about where it's heading, there's a lot of resistance and confusion. While that's understandable, it also comes from a place of not being willing to adapt.

As the way people consume content changes, and as Google is better able to qualitatively analyse sites and the content found on them, it is incumbent on us as SEOs to turn into the skid.

It also means being willing to put aside our preconceived notions and to be able to think of SEO as a more global science (or art?).

Isn't the conversation Google is having with us about expertise, authoritativeness and trustworthiness (EAT) telling us all we need to know?

The SEO world is maturing but we still seem to have a lot of focus on links and the purely technical side of search (not to demean technical SEO in any way).

I think what Google is really asking us to do is just think less about that, and more about the site itself as an entity and as a brand.

THREE THINGS YOU SHOULD DO EVERY DAY

For me, this 'ask', should really inspire people who work in SEO to do three things every day, which I'll explain in terms of my work at Wix.

First and foremost, it means being able to look at a site or a product, and not be afraid to ask how it can be improved. It also means thinking of the site and the product as a 'story', as having its own identity. I don't mean the roadmap. It's about asking what this means in terms of perception and storyline.

The second thing I do every day is to sell that story internally. It's on us as SEOs to share how we see the story of our brand and our product on the SERP. Meaning, we need to create buy-in. We need to be able to show that, by creating a strong identity around the product and brand, we will be able to seize new organic opportunities.

For many, this is a new way of thinking about organic performance and we need to do some work internally to educate people. At Wix, we have an audience that responds very well to traditional marketing so advocating for organic growth can be tricky. This outlook means fewer 'hacks', and a stronger focus on building identity and brand authority.

So, share how SEO is changing with your company – and share it with everyone. Here, I work with all sorts of teams and all sorts of different people. It's important they all understand your vision and why your perhaps less 'exciting' and less tangible growth outlook is so valuable.

The third thing I do each day is to engage with the SEO community. That could be responding to somebody who has a question about Wix on Twitter, or a podcast interview about what's going on from an SEO point of view. At the same time, it can just mean interacting with people in my industry.

There's no substitute for actually engaging with whatever industry your company finds itself in. If we're talking about SEO from the perspective of creating site and brand identity (and subsequently, authority) then you need to understand what that means in terms of your industry. No amount of keyword research or competitor analysis can replace that.

Identity and differentiation go hand-in-hand. The only way to really create that strong identity, that both users and search engines love, is to be in touch with your industry. That's not something that traditional SEO data can do for you.

THE GOOGLE QUESTION

I don't think about Google independently of my other considerations. It's all one big picture. Google is just one part of the overall audience that I'm trying to work with.

That's why it bothers me when I see people saying SEO is all about writing for the search engine and optimising content for certain users. Especially given the way that I think the algorithm works now – when you segment like that you create things that are not natural, or that are not really as effective as they could be to either audience (bots or people).

This brings me back to my real theme – if you keep on thinking like this, you're going to miss out on the real goal of SEO – growth.

You need to think about SEO in terms of brand. Where does SEO fit into creating a stronger brand identity? You need to forget optimising everything for a second and instead ask what you'd do if you were the in-house SEO but also responsible for the brand overall..

So, you have a page to work on. You need to add alt tags, images, and more. You can easily break it down into menial tasks. Or you can think about why you're creating that content.

Only when you ask that question will you create content that fosters site identity and authority. And when you create that content, then you'll be aligned with how Google's algorithm actually works.

NUANCED CONTENT IS AUTHORITATIVE CONTENT

My personal epiphany around this happened at Rank Ranger. I put a lot of work into trying to understand what verticals tend to get hit hard by a Google update.

I tracked millions of keywords. I was all about the 'big data'. And we were producing a ton of content around this. As a result, we ranked really well when an algorithm update came out. I'd do my analysis, write something up and, just like that, I was ranking on page one.

Then I asked myself, why? I had optimised the page correctly, of course, but what had really happened is that I had created a strong identity in the eyes of both users and Google. By showing expertise in a certain area and creating very authoritative content.

I'm not saying to ignore the basics. You have to have a good page structure, obviously, you shouldn't block the page from Google crawling it. But it means always thinking about SEO in terms of brand.

How do I differentiate my brand from a competitor? It's going to be through nuanced content. Google knows this – and that's where I think Google Passages is coming from.

To be able to understand the nuance of a page, so as to be able to offer users really detailed content.

The immediate response from some SEOs was to say 'we should double down on page structure and make content as structured as possible with really distinct headers and subheads'.

I take the opposite view – I think Google wants to be able to find those gems that it knows are in your longform or less optimised content. Having the structure can help, but it's also about Google being able to better understand things where there isn't that structure.

The way forward for SEO for me is to listen to the music coming out of Google and to understand that it is good content that people want to consume that matters.

At the same time, never forget your job is to help the business to meet real business targets. Data, links, ranking, yes – they matter. But they are not the priority.

Helping grow the brand is.

SEEING THE TRUE VALUE OF SEO – BY UNDERSTANDING THE BUSINESSES YOU'RE WORKING WITH

MARK PRESTON

HEAD OF DIGITAL, HAKIM GROUP

Mark has built and run agencies in the digital-marketing, and SEO, industry for 20 years.

Three years ago, he moved in-house as head of search for Hakim Group, then becoming the head of digital, at what he says is the company he will work at until he retires.

The reason for this is the fun he's having building an in-house team to manage 100-plus individual brands – and outranking the 'big boys' with a tiny budget.

You will have almost certainly interacted with the company I work for, but I bet you don't recognise the name Hakim Group (HG).

That's because we are a portfolio brand that brings together a large number of independent local opticians, and indeed, are the largest group of independent opticians in the UK.

We offer practitioners the ability to run their own business, with the freedom normally enjoyed by independents, while simultaneously providing the rigour and back-office support that usually gives bigger, high-street chains a competitive edge.

This structure has big implications for SEO. We aren't promoting a single identity because each optician has its own independent brand. At the same time, we're competing against big brands with deep pockets, the likes of Vision Express and Specsavers.

For those big players, SEO is almost a matter of clicking their fingers and spending £50,000 to test out an idea. We don't have that privilege.

So how do we compete? It's a bit of a cliche, but it's what every business needs to do in such a situation – rather than throwing money at things – we have to work a lot smarter.

THROWING OUT THE CHECKLIST

Smarter doesn't mean taking shortcuts. I'm sorry to disappoint, but there is no 'secret sauce' for good SEO. It's honestly just about doing things right and paying attention to the bits that can be quite boring.

I feel like 80 percent of the SEO industry is looking for the quickest ways of doing things, but that's not how you get a quality result. Having dedication to the business you're in is a much better strategy.

That's why we've been very careful to establish processes that are based on my long experience in the industry, and which I think are a lot better than what agencies would do for us.

Immediately prior to HG, I was running a very successful SEO training company, something I really enjoyed. The first engagement I had with the HG management team was to come and do some knowledge transfer. That all changed when I saw the opportunity here.

I joined the company soon after, with a goal to build our in-house team, because there was nobody in-house with experience of optimising content and sites. I'd done it many times and so soon after recruiting a skilled team of 15 people, my next job was creating a structure that spelled out in detail all the online processes that should be followed when a new practice becomes part of the group.

Three years later and this process, which involves everything digital that the new practice needs to do, is very well established.

BUILDING ON THEIR INDIVIDUAL STRENGTHS

At the heart of our strategy is an understanding that each optician's practice has a different demographic, a different customer. One might be in the middle of London, the next might be in a small village in Lancashire. One might focus on designer spectacles, the other may be more community-led.

We're not comparing like with like here, so we treat each of them as an individual, rather than working from a checklist. For me – checklists are destroying the industry and turning people into SEO robots.

Many of the practices have good brand awareness, not least because they might have been around for 30 or even 100 years. But these are optometrists, not digital people, and so by joining HG, they can have a digital practice up and running very quickly.

When a new practice joins, it is very rare that their website and digital presence is on point. Nearly always, the website is totally outdated and has not been touched for the past 12 years.

But the more interesting question is, now that they are competing online in their local market with the multiples and other independents, how can they beat them?

Success comes from playing to the strength of their established, local brand, and there hasn't been one single practice where we haven't increased their exposure by doing this.

From an SEO perspective, that's ranking number one, and driving new patient appointments and new business. That's our metric of SEO success. So, if you type, 'Opticians [Location]' into your search and our branch is number one, above the big brands, that's fantastic.

However, that's just the start of the journey. You need to make sure people are booking, too.

In terms of tools or approaches to get people to that front door, I can't say we're using anything special – that's the secret of our success. We use the same tools everyone else probably does: Sitebulb, Ahrefs, Semrush.

The basics aren't what makes the difference – it's what we do with them in a very particular way. Our process maps everything out very precisely.

We also direct focus when we need to, rather than working on a billable-hours basis like an agency would. If a new practice comes on board and we need to spend 30 hours in the first month working on their visibility, that's what we do. I think that's a big advantage of being in-house working on brands we own.

We can, and do, jump in a car to see them. We have our own video team that goes to take videos and photographs. We have a real connection with these practices. When it comes to SEO, that's another beauty of being in-house.

Agencies get a month to do the client work as profitably as they can. You can't really go full pelt in that scenario, whereas we can, so we do what's needed to drive new patients through their front door.

Another problem within the industry is there are lots of 'SEO things' that people just don't realise will help. There's a big focus on data, and how can we manipulate things into working for us. But that's missing the point – the key is truly understanding that new business.

What we need visitors to do is to see a practice as they would in real life. They walk through the virtual door and see a digital experience that should resemble everything they would see in the shop.

CREATING GROUP SUCCESS

So is all this hard work paying off? Well, over half of the whole group is now ranking number one in their local areas for their key terms, beating the multiples and the big brands.

But for us, the whole point of the digital and the SEO teams is to get people to walk through that front door. Once they walk through it, they should understand what to expect next, who's going to greet them, and so on. And this must reflect the individual brand. If the culture's one with a bit of a bubbly personality, that's what they have a right to expect.

I think there's a real disconnect between this kind of great user experience and the focus on data. The temptation is just to concentrate on getting highly ranked for a keyword we know people search for with regard to their eyes.

But we need to think about the patients who are the customers. What does this unique business actually have for that customer? It's about connection and it has to be about understanding the business you're doing the SEO work for. Once you do that, the plan for that particular practice naturally maps itself out.

I'd much rather have a link to the local audience where business owners are, such as their local newspaper, than in an industry publication like 'Optometry Today'. That's because I know where my target audience is and that's how I'm going to generate new business.

WHAT I SEE NOW WHEN AGENCIES PITCH ME – AND WHAT I'D RATHER SEE

I've worked both sides of the 'street' here, and only been in-house here for three years. But I do notice how differently I view in-house versus agency thinking when it comes to SEO. When an agency or a vendor comes in to pitch to me now, what I end up seeing, is just the fancy graphics and essentially meaningless promises, backed up by nothing more than unrelated case studies.

Agencies would have greater impact with me if they fully understood the company's goals and objectives for asking them to come in and pitch in the first place.

What is important to the person holding the purse strings? What mindset is the company's CEO in? What is truly important for them?

For us, the objective is to drive new patient growth. If you come in saying 'we'll write you 10 pieces of content here, we'll do this or that', it's not relevant if it doesn't align with that objective.

You are pitching X amount per month, to pay you, we'd have to generate X+Y number of appointments before we would get a decent ROI. How are you going to do that? And what happens with the retainer if you don't achieve that X+Y? Or only 50 percent of the target?

SEOs should never guarantee anything. I do understand the agency will try its best, but it's got all sorts of overheads and profit margins.

Agencies absolutely have a place, in terms of specialist skills, or in our case, coming in to train up an in-house function. And of course, there will be occasions when your skills complement what we're trying to do.

The best way forward? Agencies should always present themselves as being a useful extension to the in-house team. You're not an outsider, you add to the business' SEO capability. if you do that, and do the work to understand what's important for that business, then real synergy and progress can finally start to happen.

USING SEO TO HELP MY COMPANY PIVOT DURING LOCKDOWN

DAN RAWLEY

SEO SPECIALIST - INTERNATIONAL AND START-UPS, TWINKL EDUCATIONAL PUBLISHING

Journalism graduate Dan moved into SEO just three years ago but has built up a strong CV already, working both agency-side and in-house.

Shortlisted for Young Digital Marketer of the Year at the Northern Digital Awards, he joined specialist educational publisher Twinkl two years ago to build SEO capability from the ground up.

When I moved from an agency to an in-house SEO role, I didn't know what to expect, or where to start.

I'm based in Sheffield, and I'd just graduated and was working for a local agency when Twinkl contacted me to say they wanted me to lead a young in-house team.

Twinkl, which makes classroom resources for multiple markets around the world, managed to do very well for nine years without ever doing any SEO work – particularly as it's a digital-only business.

It had almost a decade's worth of great resources available, having employed hundreds of former teachers to develop them, but when I started, there was no SEO capacity here at all, so I knew we would make an impact no matter what we did.

Thousands of teachers were already visiting the website every year and they would sign up, buy a subscription and then download as many resources as they wanted, printing them out at home or at school to use in their classrooms. But, because there was no SEO, the company wasn't doing particularly well on Google and didn't show up for many search phrases.

The brand had fallen behind all its competitors, who had been investing in SEO for years, and although the UK website is the most popular by far, as we operate multiple websites for other countries, we would need SEO on all those sites, too.

Twinkl's year-on-year traffic had gradually declined, and the company wanted to turn it around so that in 2019 it would see 20 percent higher traffic than the year before.

In a very short space of time, we have transformed an underused section of the site to bring in 1.3 million organic sessions a year. And we've built up an SEO team from scratch to become what I think is an industry leading company.

SEO is now a top priority for this 500-person strong organisation – and the CEO is our biggest fan.

GRASPING THE OPPORTUNITY

I think any SEO will immediately see this was a massive opportunity and thankfully the management realised that too.

I came in as SEO team leader in March 2019, as part of a team of five, which is a pretty normal size for in-house SEO. After that, it just grew and grew, because there was so much work to do. We now have 15 people on the team and we're still growing.

We needed all those extra pairs of hands because there was nine years of content and thousands of pages that needed SEO work, as well as some stiff targets to meet.

It initially seemed very ambitious, in terms of what SEO could do, but in the end, we hit our 20 percent target quite comfortably. We actually saw a 70 percent increase in traffic from 2018 to 2019.

Because of the amount of time Twinkl had been around, there were already some search phrases it showed up for, but to boost our traffic, we did a lot more keyword research. I found Semrush and SEO Monitor great for finding new keywords that we currently didn't rank for and we quickly surfaced the lucrative ones that lots of people were using.

Of course, our CEO also wanted to see an increase in revenue coming in through search engines, so we had to crack that.

The problem with the website was that we had thousands of amazing teacher resources, but you couldn't find them unless you were already on it. The site had a million pages, but the brand wasn't making the most of that content because we had a paywall in place to stop people just taking our content. This meant there was nothing for search engines to look up, because the site didn't describe what was in the resource.

All we had to do for some of the most popular resources was write really descriptive information that showed search engines what it was all about. We also did a lot of work coming up with more automated ways of improving content visibility, like writing code to add phrases to the title of every page that we didn't have time to update manually.

Basically, we put a lot of hard work into making us more visible and maximising our SEO. We were powering along ... and then lockdown hit.

HOME-LEARNING NEW SEO STRATEGIES DURING LOCKDOWN

When all UK children got sent home and schools were closed, it hugely disrupted our processes.

Traditionally, we used keyword research to find out that, say, 1,000 people per month were looking for a specific teaching resource. And we'd know immediately to target 'key stage two maths worksheets' for example.

Now, we were all home learning – and there was demand for resources that we didn't necessarily have. This was obviously a completely new situation and so of course the teaching materials needed to be different to the past.

We quickly realised lots of people now searching for resources weren't teachers, but parents and guardians suddenly finding themselves in the role of home-school teaching.

Our old, monthly averages for keyword research went out the window – no one was looking for maths worksheets anymore – instead it was 'home learning', 'help for parents' and so on.

For a short while, the team that produces our classroom resources were not quite sure what to start work on.

Luckily, we had Google Trends, which we hadn't used very much up until then. And another tip for other in-house SEOs, and something I'm very proud of is, is using Google Trends and a little bit of lateral thinking.

I use Google Trends to spot demand for a new product in other markets before the UK has even started to search for it. This means that we're totally set up and ahead of all our competitors when people do start searching.

Here, I could see that this would be a great way of keeping up with what people were searching for around home-schooling during the pandemic.

However, while Google Trends shows you what people are searching for today, which is really useful, sometimes, it's almost too late, because it takes a couple of days to make a new resource, and by that time, someone else has made it, or the demand has moved on.

Things were very fast moving in the market at the start of the pandemic.

LOOKING FOR INTERNATIONAL INSPIRATION

To get ahead, we decided to look at the countries that had gone into lockdown before us, like Italy and Spain.

I thought that, if we could get insights into what people were searching for, that might be what people would want here in a few weeks. Then, by the time demand in the UK caught up, we would already have made all these resources ready to go.

We did this for lots of our resources, but the one that sticks in my mind is one we made after we saw demand in Spain for a personalised certificate that rewards a child for good behaviour. It's a really simple thing to make, but no one in the UK wanted that yet, because we hadn't been in lockdown for long enough that parents thought they would need it.

I fed the idea back to the production team, they made it and it did really well. Between April and December 2020, the certificate had more than 7,000 downloads and over 32,000 pageviews. The vast majority of these were in the two weeks after the resources went live.

That's not bad for a product created based on an opportunity we wouldn't have spotted without SEO. It was also syndicated out to different markets, so we made one for Australia, New Zealand and the US, with France and Romania having just gone live, too.

USING SEO IN A CRISIS

I think that's a genuinely great example of how SEO can help you get ahead of the curve, with products ready to go before people realise that they want them. So if there is some sort of crisis that upsets how the business runs normally, SEO can be the department that finds a solution.

I don't think people consider that SEO is something that can lead a business. But we showed the CEO how SEO was able to help the company stay ahead of what was going on, even during a crisis.

HOW TO AVOID BAD DECISIONS IN YOUR FIRST PROCUREMENT PROCESS? BE PREPARED – AND BE HONEST

RIC RODRIGUEZ

SEARCH DIRECTOR AT VASHI

Ric Rodriguez was a co-author of the first Mastering In-House SEO book last year, when he was the European search-marketing expert at the NYSE-listed technology firm Yext.

Given his wide experience as client, agency and vendor, Ric – who's now Search Director at the fine-jewellery brand Vashi – continues on the theme of collaboration. Here he explains how you can create meaningful relationships with your partners, creating value for everyone.

As marketers, we need our brilliant partners. Whether for data, reporting, or to action projects for us, we often collaborate with a number of different businesses to deliver on our objectives.

Selecting the right partnerships – and setting them up to succeed – is an important part of overseeing any in-house channel. But, managing a vendor relationship is often something we're not exposed to until it's expected of us – and the learning curve can lead to us making avoidable, unfortunate decisions.

I could write a book on this topic, but here, we'll be focussing on one important part – the beginning.

An effective selection process is key to creating a valuable partnership – and making a considered decision can set you up for the long term. The challenge is that many search marketers aren't skilled negotiators and have never had formal procurement training.

This, combined with a generally negative perception of vendor-sales teams (perhaps from feeling 'bombarded' with lead-generation emails or cold calls), can make the process feel inhospitable.

But it need not be – and putting yourself in the shoes of the salesperson – may lead you to a more insightful product demo, a more robust business case and ultimately, a better deal.

Like every great story, the path to your next partnership has a beginning (discovery), a middle (the selling) and an end (the negotiation). My key advice is to be honest and open throughout.

THE 'DISCOVERY PHASE' – EMPOWERING THEM TO SAY 'NO'

Almost every sale, whether it's from a cold call or when you're proactively reaching out, starts with a process of discovery ('fact finding'), which is used to tailor the pitch to you. If the first call is only an hour, I would expect – as the prospect – to do most of the talking.

I always recommend coming prepared. What are your challenges? What are you hoping a platform will help you do? What does 'great' look like? And, importantly, what's your decision-making process and timeline?

Being asked questions, when you're expecting a features and functionality discussion, may feel like a time drain, but this process does two things for you. Firstly, it enables them to have better future discussions with you. Secondly, it actually saves time (and money), as you'll receive a response that clearly answers your brief.

In an ideal world, if a potential partner can't meet your requirements, they should say so – and at least – you've empowered them to do so. It may be that they can meet some, but not others.

Either way, enter the next phase with an open mind and be prepared to be challenged – if the solution was easy, you'd have likely already done it yourself.

An important next step here is often to share a non-disclosure agreement, which can also act as a tool to create space in the communications for you to explore them independently before moving forward in the process.

THE '(VALUE) SELLING PHASE' – MATCHING THE SOLUTION TO WHAT YOU NEED

It's important to know your 'must haves' versus 'nice to haves', as this will help you move the conversation forward as a potential partner starts to bring you deeper into their world.

But, at this stage, some flexibility can be helpful, too. Do consider speed and expectations – particularly if the solution you're exploring is complex – it's unrealistic to think you'll evaluate it in one single sitting.

The discussion will often need more information to proceed and, before investing their resources, a salesperson will want a sense of your appetite. In this case, if something is particularly important to you, be open to further scoping. Systems aren't binary and some parts may suit you better than others – a great solution is one that is specific to you and does what you need it to do, not what it says on the tin.

Here, we should consider the role of a 'solutions engineer', also called a 'sales engineer', who is a technical-product expert. While they may demo the product, it's not uncommon for them to be solely involved with scoping out more complex projects. Their time is often very limited, so don't be offended if you're not offered an opportunity to speak to them at the start.

It's important not to see them as 'more salespeople'. While many have been through sales training, their objective is to demonstrate that the system aligns with your requirements. Their goal is not to pitch to you, but they can offer ideas, advice and guidance.

And they're often thinking about the long term, so don't be afraid to ask how they see the system enduring, or about the upcoming-features roadmap. Solutions engineers will have the best technical knowledge of anyone on the sales team, so if you are able to speak to one, bring your most complex questions forward.

Sales teams also often have access to some incredible resources, so they can help you create business cases, get buy-in from your stakeholders and push the boundaries of what you believe is possible. If you're bought into what's being sold, you could even set up higher-level meetings with senior people you need on board.

Above all, try to build a good rapport with your partners. Ultimately, we're all human, trying to do what's best for our businesses, so mutual respect not only makes the process far more enjoyable, it can lead to a less-stressful negotiation and ongoing relationship.

THE 'NEGOTIATION PHASE' – CLOSING A DEAL THAT WORKS FOR EVERYONE

You've reached the point where you like the solution and it aligns with your requirements. Now we have the small task of agreeing a price – which shouldn't be difficult for either side.

There's a simple fact here. If you push hard for a discount, you're going to lose value. Most partners can offer a reduction, either because you're buying at scale, or perhaps because you've built a great relationship. Generally there's a level that salespeople can offer, a level for local sales management and then – for the biggest deals – one signed off by an executive (such as the chief revenue officer).

How hard to push is a delicate balance between knowing there is some movement and making an unrealistic price a non-negotiable. On the latter, the only way your partner will be able to meet you is to reduce services – and you'll find things like support levels disappear. That isn't a discount, it's a worse deal.

But if pricing is important to you, there are some levers you can pull, by understanding the drivers behind sales success. Salespeople work to targets (as do the businesses behind them), so as you get closer to the end of a reporting period, such as a sales quarter, you may be able to negotiate a better rate for signing before this..

This can be a great move for everyone, but it's only worth suggesting if you're confident your legal and procurement teams can meet this pace – otherwise you may do more harm than good.

The best approach is to look at 'add-ons' versus 'cutbacks'. It may be that they can offer enhanced support, better access to data, or increase reporting frequency at no added cost, if you agree a certain price. The great thing here is that you're getting additional (and bespoke) value, that doesn't come at a major cost to your partner – a win for both parties.

Moreover, if these additional services include a limited number of features from a higher product or support tier, you may be able to negotiate these into a future sales opportunity – where you can show results before agreeing an additional cost.

Finally there is the contract itself – and usually my advice is to keep out of the legal aspect. But, you can always help your team by doing a 'first pass' to find points of contention (your 'red lines').

If your brand will only accept certain payment terms (the amount of time after an invoice is due before costs are incurred), or has a stance on 'auto-renewals' or notice clauses, you can make these clear before a contract is put forward. This cuts the back and forth, so it's always worth knowing your policies in these areas.

Also, remember that some contract terms can impact prices – a two-year deal will often have an economy of scale applied over a one-month rolling deal. I recommend – as you did with the solution itself – thinking about the contract terms before you start negotiating – and being honest. If you need something to come in at a certain price, work with your salesperson to see if things can be changed, offers applied or value added.

At most levels of business, you'll be able to shape the contract and the final terms can be as unique as the solution you're buying.

A FINAL THOUGHT FROM SOMEONE WHO HAS SEEN EVERY SIDE

Setting up a prospective partner for success comes down to two things – preparation and honesty. By being honest and prepared about your challenges and your non-negotiables and your selection process, this will help you meaningfully assess the options. This will make your decision easier and ultimately deliver the best possible outcome for your business, and your partners, creating the basis for a mutually successful relationship.

It's in nobody's interest for a deal to fail, as time and effort goes into building the processes around it, and it's daunting because you're making a decision that'll impact you for a month, a year or longer.

A service or product agreement should be as unique as the solution it's there to solve – and both sides need to understand the challenge – in order to build a long-standing relationship.

WHETHER ADOPTING THE LATEST SOFTWARE OR ACQUIRING ANOTHER BRAND'S WEBSITE – A BAD MIGRATION IS SOMETHING YOU MIGHT NEVER RECOVER FROM

ROMAN SADOWSKI

SEO ACCOUNT MANAGER, IPROSPECT

Now at iProspect, Roman has led the SEO charge at Irish children's toy and entertainment products multinational Smyths Toys Superstores for six years.

His work has included no-less-than three full website migrations, including acquiring Toys R Us' Central Europe site, which saw him dealing with 20,000 301 redirects, as well as close liaison with the development team on SEO website optimisation, from 404 management to implementing hreflang, meta

---

At time of interview Roman was Senior SEO Lead at Smyths Toys Superstores

When the opportunity at Smyths came up, I immediately thought how amazing it was to be in a company growing as fast as it was, going from local to multinational in a very short time.

I also really liked the flexibility and energy of the company. It was all very small teams and the management were always highly accessible. It really was a unique environment.

And from my experience, I know that SEO can contribute to a fast-growing consumer brand like Smyths. My SEO strategy was a major contributor to the company's strong organic growth from 2014 onwards – which in 2020 – saw Smyths ranked number 14, with the largest SEO growth in the UK, out of 250 brands.

To make this happen, I implemented a number of SEO content strategies that ended up with us outranking all Smyths's direct competition.

I also managed some major website migrations and I think what I learned here is something other SEOs will get particular value out of.

A lot of site migrations are driven by company growth outpacing the technology of the time. At Smyths, we had to catch up with the way people wanted to shop, which kept changing, and to the demand from customers – so we needed to keep moving from one major piece of software to the next.

I might not need to tell anyone in SEO what a huge undertaking it is to move your whole website, especially one of any size, to yet another platform and to have everything migrate perfectly. But I'd go so far as to say SEO is the most important factor that needs to be considered when doing website migrations.

My approach to getting SEO website migrations right doesn't involve any 'secrets', I'm afraid. It's always just a lot of painstaking work. It's also one challenge if it's your brand moving from one domain to the same domain on a different platform, but it's totally different when you acquire a website and you're trying to merge that one with your own.

MAKING SURE GOOGLE DOESN'T NOTICE YOU'RE MOVING

The last time I had to get in the weeds with a migration was when our company acquired Toys R Us' Central European operations. As part of the package, we bought the website, which was still live, so we had to take that brand, and redirect it to our own platform and domain. And it was really important we did this well, so that Google wouldn't notice there'd been a change.

Firstly, with an external brand, you don't really know what you are merging, so it's really important that you take the time to find out every single piece of information about that domain. Because, if there's bad stuff on that website, you don't want to inject that into yours.

Take care to screen everything thoroughly using tools like Screaming Frog to establish what links you want to disavow and to identify the lower-quality content you don't want.

Next, you have to really look at the redirects, and be clear that you can't just leave this to the development team – they don't have the necessary expertise and their instinct is to just link to the homepage.

Automatically creating a rule that every page from one domain gets redirected to the homepage is not really maximising the future outcome in Google. The reality is – you have to do it page by page.

30 YEARS OF AUTHORITY BUILT IN

There were 10,500 pages to map from the Toys R Us site, so this was not an easy job. But more important was that, even though we were incorporating content from a not-great website that was nearly 30 years old, it still had a lot of authority built in.

It was a massive toy brand and people were still landing on those pages, so it had traffic and an audience that we wanted to capture, to turn those visitors into our customers. For example, we wanted to make the old Toys

R Us Barbie page redirect to our Smyths Toys' Barbie page. To do this, we had to tell the developers to put it all on the servers and test the hell out of it before we went live.

We were hampered somewhat in that I also had to manage the Toys R Us team and they didn't have any data because the site had always been managed from the US. Even though I didn't have this, I got a lot of value out of Google Analytics, Ahrefs and Screaming Frog.

I also needed to pull a lot of information about how the website was structured from the old Toys R Us Central European SAP system, but the whole thing was dynamically generated, so it was challenging just to get the list of website pages.

All in all, the project took three months, which I understand is very fast.

LEARNING ON THE JOB

You have to accept that you can't test some things in Google, because it can't 'see' all the pages until you press the 'go' button. You just have to plan for there being issues that you didn't foresee, then, when Google starts to crawl the website and spots all the errors, you have to work through those too. So there are a few months after going live where you're fixing any issues.

The redirect was important because we could use it to learn about customer behaviour. We were expecting that people who used to buy toys from Toys R Us would be happy to buy toys from Smyths. But, because it's a new brand that isn't known to them, we needed to gain their trust by providing a great service, in order to win them as a customer.

Language was another interesting point that we didn't think about. Google in Germany picked up our UK website because it was just much stronger, so if you searched for Smyths stores in Germany, our UK website would come up, and people wouldn't click because it wasn't in German.

We had to fix that and then we saw that the click-throughs go from 6 to 60 percent. Of course you need to serve your content in the local language, or people will not buy from you – so simple, but we never thought of that.

Was it all worth it? Yes! We managed to capture all the Toys R Us traffic that was landing on these old websites, and from this, we started to record visits and sales.

OUTGROWING THE LAST MIGRATION

Two years later – we've outgrown our technology again and so we need to upgrade to the SAP Hybris platform. We need to do this to offer customers a better experience on the website, with faster, better content and a more convenient way of shopping.

Such migrations can still be a major issue for SEO for a number of reasons. One very important factor is that every one of your pages sits under a unique URL, with a unique location. And once you start to mess with that structure, you kill the first one and create another one.

This means that Google now cannot see what it had before, and all your content is in totally different locations and on totally different pages, which Google doesn't know about. So, you need to redirect all those old locations into new locations in a way Google won't notice.

For example, if you search on Google for Lego, Smyths may well have paid to get a top ranking for that, but if you delete that page and replace it with a different one, you need to make sure it does the job needed for Google to pick up the new one.

Do that 20,000 times for 20,000 pages, and it can be really risky. If 60 percent of your revenue comes in from organic traffic, you can really mess things up if you don't do a migration properly.

This isn't something you can just automate. The server redirects happen automatically, but you still need a human to evaluate both the old and new websites to ensure that you don't pass any low-quality or thin content. You also need to be confident that all the equity from inbound links is passed on to the new pages and that your customers won't ever land on broken pages.

Migrations can go really wrong on that and lose even really big brands a lot of visibility overnight, as well as lots of traffic and sales. Worse, if it is badly implemented, it's really hard to recover.

My key recommendations for successful, SEO-positive site migrations are:

- Do not redirect to the homepage only – do redirects on a per-page basis.
- Watch for the developers' inclination to set 'allowed to index' – they don't care if they index test websites, you do.
- Test, test, test, before go-live. Test everything, everything! Those redirects need to work, so make sure they do.
- Local-language issues matter. Serve content in local languages, or people won't click on your links and shoppers will not convert on your website
- It's one thing to acquire a great brand – but you still need to earn trust and that will take time.

NOW'S THE TIME TO THINK ABOUT A LONG-TERM CAREER IN SEO

ELI SCHWARTZ

GROWTH CONSULTANT AND ADVISOR

Eli spent seven successful years leading the SEO team at San Francisco-based SurveyMonkey, becoming Director of Growth in 2017.

He now works as an independent growth advisor and consultant, building on more than a decade of experience delivering global SEO strategies that dramatically increase organic visibility, at scale, for the likes of Shutterstock, WordPress, Quora and Zendesk.

He is also the author of Product Led SEO.

Are you ready for a heretical statement? *I don't believe in in-house SEO.*

What I believe in is marketing and product leaders. Because, when you pigeonhole yourself as an 'in-house SEO', your career gets stunted. This means you either have to move to a really big company if you want to get paid more, or you want to secure a better job title. Or you just move out of SEO.

I don't say this to upset anyone, but there are just a finite number of things you can achieve in an in-house SEO role. I've been there. I spent many years in this field and I've recruited many other people into it too. Ask yourself, 'are you doing anything differently on day 500 versus day one?'.

I think, if you're honest with yourself, you're still optimising pages. You might be better at it, but you're still essentially optimising content.

And the only ways to change that are to create something different that moves the needle, or by creating something completely new. Then you can say, 'hey folks, I built out this entire suite of web pages or products!'. Otherwise, it's 'last year I optimised those 100 pages... and this year I optimised these 100 pages'.

THREE OPTIONS FOR GETTING OUT OF THIS DEAD END

To liberate yourself from this dead end, you need to be working with your brand's product team to help them build something that adds value to the business. They're the ones that own the website, so if you aren't giving them useful SEO insights and changing the focus of pages they're building, what difference are you really making?

To me, there are three ways to advance.

First – open your eyes, and look at the people in your company – especially peers who seem to be more successful or better paid than you. Listen to how they speak and see what they're doing differently.

In my case, I noticed it was the product people. They received more respect because they created things. They were able to command engineers and got promoted when they did well. They could take credit for things they did, because it was the engineers that physically built them. I realised that if I changed my terminology and my approach to sound more like them, I would be more successful. And it worked.

Second – speak the language that everyone else speaks in your organisation. If everyone else is talking about revenue or downloads or pageviews, then use those terms and those metrics.

I say this because, too often in SEO, people struggle to make comparisons, or say, 'it depends'. Making everything 'apples with apples' means your work is directly comparable to the work anyone else is doing.

For example, if the marketing team says that they spent $2 million and generated $2 million plus one cent, to them that's a huge success. If you respond by pointing out that you didn't make any money, but you generated 'this many' rankings, it's impossible to make a direct comparison.

But if you can say, 'I spent $100 on SEO and here's how much money we made as a result', that's comparing apples with apples, and your apple is the shinier one.

Third – take credit for everything you do. Stop saying things like, 'as part of my job, I asked the content writer to...'. Rather than saying that you helped the engineer build a new thing, say that you built it – and asked the engineer to help. Say that you came up with a new content idea and got the content person to write it for you.

This is the language of successful people in companies. In smaller companies, you do a good job, or you get fired. In bigger companies, speaking the language of success and not fading into the background are the keys to advancement.

SEOS NEED TO STOP BEING WALLFLOWERS

I want you as an SEO to stand at the front of the room. I want you to run up there and be ahead of those other marketers.

SEO is not a 'support function' at all. At SurveyMonkey, two thirds of the company's revenue was driven by SEO. Why should I fade into the background when I was the biggest revenue driver there?

Salespeople get cheered, and patted on the back, and given gold rings every time they close a deal. But as an SEO, you're driving revenue of equal or greater value, every hour. So take credit for the things you do.

My final piece of advice? What SEOs really need is extreme confidence. Whether you're in-house or a consultant, if you're not confident, why should they pay you the big bucks? If they ask you a question and you keep answering, 'it depends', they'll ask someone that will give them an answer.

If you go to a doctor and ask, 'is this cancer?' and the doctor says, 'well...', you don't leave the office satisfied with what you learned. People don't like to pay people who say it depends.

So be extremely confident. Lean towards the outcome that is most likely. You won't always be right, but no one ever is in business.

When I pitch to a major global organisation, I don't get the contract unless I go in and say, 'you're going to pay me to tell you what to do. I might not always be right, but I will tell you what to do'. That's what they pay people for.

So whether you're in-house or an agency SEO, your job is to be confident in what you know. And if you're lacking confidence, do the research to get it.

It's this that will help you be the leader you want to be.

CHOOSING TO GET INTO SEO

Everyone says they 'fell into' SEO, and so did I, but I was very deliberately falling.

I was working at a lead-generation company that helped small businesses generate leads, whether it was for a new mortgage, or insurance, or to fix their windows. We were all about matching up businesses with people that wanted a service. How we did that was by partnering with people who had websites that were good at driving traffic, whether paid or primarily organic.

I was working with these affiliates and we were writing them cheques for $50,000 a month because they had websites. It wasn't long before I started to think, 'I don't like my job – I like their job!'.

I would hit all the numbers I needed to do for my day job, then I spent time learning what my affiliates were doing. I reverse engineered their websites, learning about things like backlinks, and I read all the guides (I still recommend Aaron Wall's book on SEO, which I read cover to cover).

Then I started building my own websites – and from that moment on – all I did was apply for SEO jobs. So, I did sort of fall into it, but I was also very deliberate about this being what I wanted to do.

Everything I have done since then has been about enhancing my potential to work as an SEO consultant.

YOUR SEO CONFIDENCE IN ACTION

I have the kind of confidence I am talking about here because I know I've made a difference.

Recently, I was contacted by a public company that does a couple of billion dollars a year in sales. They spend tens of millions of dollars per month on paid advertising on Facebook and Google, but they have not driven any SEO traffic.

They were willing to allocate all funds possible towards unlocking an SEO opportunity – and the question they had was, 'how do we do that?'. They had all this money, and engineers and product people standing by, and they needed us to tell them what to do.

I quickly lined up all the potential areas where they could build SEO, then prioritised the ones that were doable fast.

Keep in mind that this was a publicly traded company and everything they do is under scrutiny. Changing the 'title' tag meant that legal had to sign off on that change. Updating an image meant they had to go back and see if they were allowed to do it.

This was probably the stickiest challenge I've ever had to work on, but luckily for me the team was extremely fast moving.

The company could easily have written hundreds of blog posts targeting the primary terms in their industry. They already had hundreds of blog posts, but they hadn't worked.

They had driven millions of visits from search, but they didn't convert, because they had written the posts without a clear SEO strategy.

We developed what our product was going to be, how we could build something in their industry that would drive the traffic that would click their 'calls to action' and be in the market to buy what this product was selling.

The client had to see that being successful wasn't about writing blog posts, because they had already done that, but that being successful is about building something brilliant and tying those pieces together.

The takeaway for me is that, too often, companies do things they call 'SEO', but they've really just asked someone to do some keyword research and write some blog posts.

A list of keywords is not a strategy – and they don't have any metrics.

It's much better to adopt product-led SEO, which means creating something useful for the visitor, using research to develop a 'search product'. If my user research is correct, my search product will follow, and I'll be creating search volume around what I've created.

I think it's more useful to think about someone's needs and intentions rather than thinking about what keywords they're punching in. I hit the 'Holy Grail' when I create meaning – once the idea exists others start looking for it – the keyword research. And

SEO IS A CRAFT – AND IN-HOUSE SEOS NEED TO PROFESSIONALISE IT FAST – OR WE'LL MAKE OURSELVES OBSOLETE

DOMINIK SCHWARZ

CHIEF INBOUND OFFICER, HOMETOGO/VERTICAL INHOUSE

Dominik started building websites when he was 13 and founded an early web-hosting company, so is a highly experienced digital practitioner.

His long history of working in the online industry spans corporate and agency roles, working on SEO alongside marketing and strategy.

He now heads up inbound marketing as Chief Inbound Officer at holiday-rentals leader HomeToGo, alongside leading Vertical Inhouse, an organisation that provides resources for in-house SEOs.

As a longstanding champion of in-house SEO, this year he's revisited his call for greater professionalisation within our sector – with an even greater sense of urgency.

As an in-house SEO – you know you need to keep learning. You need to know what's important now and what will be important in the future.

We tend to do this by going to conferences and speaking with experts – and that's great.

But we need to give far greater prominence to the career and business aspects of the job. Because our understanding of the 'political' aspect of SEO – the tough, necessary work of pushing something through an organisation until it gets done – is still lacking.

SEO is much more than 'just technology' or applying some knowledge to improving the company website.

Being an effective SEO means having a good understanding of corporate politics, knowing how to shape an organisation and educate the business. Not to mention budgeting and managing suppliers. These things actually account for the majority of the average SEO's day, though you'd never know that from reading the (SEO) books.

Maybe 10 or 15 years ago, success was easy, because everything to do with the internet was far less complex. The internet was much smaller, there was a 'Wild West' feel to it and many people built their careers in that period.

Today, technical knowledge is only a fraction of what SEOs need to do to succeed. That's why the next chapter for our industry has to be about the professionalisation of in-house SEO.

IT'S ABOUT EXECUTION – NOT SECRETS

Like everything on the Internet, SEO has certainly moved on. By applying better technology and testing frameworks, and doing all the technical work, we've extended SEO to a far higher intellectual and scientific level. There's also great software out there.

But in a lot of ways, digital marketing, and SEO in particular, still wear cowboy hats. I say this because there are still people saying things like, 'no, I can't tell you these special SEO secrets in my possession'.

Our whole industry is still holding tightly to this idea that there are 'special SEO secrets'. And that just isn't true. It's not about secrets. It's only ever about execution.

If we look around, we can see that this is very normal for the evolution of a marketing channel. Look back 70 years to when TV was emerging – in the early days of TV advertising, people had no idea about the most successful way to do that sort of thing – but this has changed and the way the industry phrases its messaging has advanced enormously.

If you accept that SEO is still a relatively new and young discipline, the problem is that we haven't taken this step yet. We are mystifying our colleagues with this pretence there's this thing called 'Google's secret knowledge'. because we are still not equipped with the right mindset.

We claim SEO is different to any other channel, that we can't predict what will happen and why. But that is true for any marketing channel that isn't purely performance driven. If I create a TV advertising spot, I don't know in advance how many people will come to our website afterwards.

But as a TV-spot producer and a CMO, I need to come up with a strong and solid prediction. Everybody understands that this is just a prediction, based on my experience and knowledge, and market data. Way too often, the SEO is claiming 'they're different and more special' than everybody else, and that really we're working for Google.

I would be the first to say that Google and its actions are a factor here. But you don't work for Google, you work for your brand. If it was really true that you have no control over what Google can do, why does your company need an SEO function at all?

It's no coincidence that a running gag in the SEO industry is, 'it depends'. And that is just not acceptable anymore.

END OUR IMMATURE 'IT DEPENDS' ATTITUDE

The reality is that most of the problems we have in SEO are not because we don't know the right thing to do. They exist because the SEO isn't trusted enough to make the necessary changes. And we shoot ourselves in the foot, by reverting to this 'Wild West' thinking.

So we need to accelerate our maturation. We need to know our data inside out and understand our own value. SEO is not a mystic art, it's a craft.

The way we start educating the organisation to the potential of search, and our contribution as SEOs, is to change how we talk to the business. We need to come to the job with a whole lot of science, but also a whole lot of strong opinions and measurability.

When an SEO talks to the CMO or the CFO or the CEO, we need to go in knowing what the business wants – which is real numbers and data that go beyond rankings.

There's more than enough information out there on best practice – a clear blueprint for success – and we see the same SEO problems on all e-commerce sites. I'd go so far as to say that the answers to 80 or 90 percent of all SEO questions are obvious. It's doing your part properly as the craftsperson that is the hard part.

So you need to have faith that your work has measurable and predictable impact.

You also need to stop being shy about being compared with other marketing channels. SEOs need to play with the 'big boys' and be taken as seriously as the TV or the PPC people. We know that SEO is consistently delivering massive value – and we should go with our heads held high into any c-suite or investor meetings – and demonstrate that.

For the brightest and smartest SEO teams out there, and the most forward-looking users of SEO, things are evolving in the right way. But this is only happening at the bigger organisations.

SMEs still tend to only hire one SEO person – and they then expect that one person to do everything related to SEO. But surely, what we've learned in the last few years, is that SEO is not a department, but a horizontal implementation in your organisational structure.

This means that a single specialist can never create the full potential value of search across the whole organisation.

EVOLVE OR DIE?

So what happens if we don't continue to evolve, to take this step?

If our profession is pigeonholed as 'just the SEO' and is seen as an appendix of the marketing department, then you have no chance to influence anything.

That includes the company's thinking on technology, content, product, brand and anything else that matters to us.

SEO will come under more and more pressure. In fact, there are already a lot of places where SEO is becoming less relevant. Google is taking away a share – our playing field is becoming smaller and we don't get the same exposure anymore.

Of course, Google is not the only player that sends us traffic. Maybe it is Pinterest, maybe it is another social media platform. Maybe it is Amazon. Maybe it is a special portal.

Really, it's our job to find and identify and claim all spaces that are available for free.

And if we start doing that and professionalise, we're going to be so much more successful in everything we're trying to achieve.

The fact remains – SEO is a craft, something that needs to be executed well

KNOWLEDGE WANTS TO BE FREE – BUT SEOS STILL NEED TO MAKE IT FINDABLE

JP SHERMAN

MANAGER OF SEARCH & FINDABILITY, RED HAT

You'd have to look pretty hard to find an SEO with a more varied career.

His CV includes spells as an amateur palaeontologist, an autopsy assistant, work in airborne special operations and as a massage therapist.

He's been happily working in SEO since 2001 and is settled in North Carolina, where he looks after search and what he calls 'findability' at enterprise software organisation Red Hat (now part of IBM).

There are many people I would consider to be better at SEO than I am. My true passion is to create natural and intuitive search experiences that connect a user's intent to the information they need. And I have a different perspective on what it means to be an in-house SEO.

At Red Hat, I use our open-source philosophy, which, plainly stated, is that information and knowledge wants to be shared. Sometimes, we just need to give it a bit of a helping hand.

From the small business to the enterprise, people use both SEO and onsite search to find what they're looking for – and my position focusses on delivering on both of those pathways.

I also have a conviction that SEOs need to keep in focus how the work they do must also improve search results for people visiting their website. For example, if a user thinks you have what they're looking for, they're likely to search your website.

However, if you haven't added keyword meta-tags because you learned that Google doesn't use them as relevancy signals, you may not know that your site-search platform likely does use keyword meta-tags.

Not considering both Google and your own platform can create unintended consequences, and people may not find what you have to offer. I firmly believe that SEO, at its foundation, must always be about understanding people and intent, including people of different backgrounds.

I try to deliver on these ideals as manager of search and findability. I help humans find the information they're looking for, regardless of the search channel they use.

I do that using SEO for sure, but I also employ on-site search, machine learning, content strategy and development, templating, architecture, platform analysis and optimisation.

The job is working out how to make it easier for people to look for, find and use the information they need on the Red Hat Customer Portal.

DON'T FORGET SITE SEARCH

There are two main Red Hat websites. The first is redhat.com, the marketing arm of the organisation where we develop open-source software for enterprise clients. There, users search for very specific keywords and content is always being developed around these to drive traffic. This site is really focused on selling the brand – and conversion.

I run all the relevancy operations for our site search, as well as all our SEO to help people find us on Google and other search engines. DuckDuckGo is really big for us.

On the portal, we help existing Red Hat clients who have very specific needs.

They may need to figure out how to set up a mailer daemon in an x64-bit bare metal environment, so they come to us for that, which is why site search is just as important, because people are using very specific pieces of software.

I love working with our marketing teams, but there's very little competition for 'how do I set up a mailer team and an X 64-bit environment'. That's why I focus on the long tail – 80 percent of keywords that drive traffic to us are three-to-five words long. So I segment by 'low frequency, high intent'.

My users are not just Red Hat enterprise clients or partners. They're going to be everything from Linux enthusiasts who use our software for free, to systems administrators and developers. We are here to serve the open-source community. Anyone who's looking to use our software is going to want to find information, and my job is to allow them to find it.

I do that focussing on this concept of 'findability' rather than 'search', because I believe that SEO is a tactic people use to put their information on search engines, but there are a lot of different ways that people find information beyond the main search engines.

We use chatbots, AI, SEO, site search, and a big component of what we do is UI/UX. I think all of these things, working together in concert, allow a human to find what they're looking for. To help, we organise our information by tasks, not just products. So if someone searches a specific product name, they'll find it, but if they don't know the name, we still want to provide information to them.

FORGET GOOGLE – DON'T FORGET THE USER

This might sound a little heretical, but this is why Google doesn't really occupy too much of my brain space. I care more about people than I care about Google.

I don't need to tell anyone in SEO that Google tends to be a little mercurial. It updates, it changes, what worked yesterday no longer works today.

So I focus on the user first. If I give them a good user experience that engenders trust, applied through the knowledge that they learn. And if my site is good, organised, topical, related to other supporting topics, then Google is going to see us and say in its clever, robotic way, 'I know what this is about and there's a wealth of information that surrounds the topic. Clearly there's expertise here'.

That doesn't mean I'm not doing technical SEO – far from it. I don't leave the optimisation for phrases and words to the marketing team. I'm on the engineering team. This means I have access to Drupal developers, people who do our Progressive Web Applications, people who have the ability to do JavaScript things.

This means I can make sure that our development is clean, our site is fast, our architecture and templates are solid, our H1s are all in the right place.

Site search is really important in all of this. Of course, I have to do this correctly for pragmatic reasons – if someone can find what they need on the site with my tool, that reinforces trust and our expertise. If they can't, Google is less than two seconds away.

So delivering a good result in site search is a huge multiplier for trust, longevity and conversion. In our case, that means driving people to our subscriptions.

Getting this right can be tricky. For example, one of our products is called Satellite, but at the start of the site search, it could be a thing out in space. We don't know yet.

The intent is probably that the user is looking for the product, but if somebody is giving us just that one word, we can't be sure we know what they're looking for.

To help, I built a Knowledge Graph that supports the natural-language results, as a multiplier to our natural search. That has increased click-through rates by 15 to 20 percent, because we're predicting what the user is looking for, then giving it to them.

The Knowledge Graph is built out of our own product, Red Hat OpenShift and we try to use our own products to build things. I use JSon, but I also use Splunk, Tableau and the Adobe analytics stack. I find Deep Crawl perfectly fits our needs, although I do groan when it tells me there are 3,000 things I need to fix.

WORKING ON FINDABILITY

Getting the right tools is a huge help because we are looking at over 1.5 million individual pieces of content, and when I first started, there was a very basic level of organisation, in that things were tagged, but there was a lot of duplicate content.

Once I found groups of duplicates, I worked with our technology teams to start paring off the dead branches. Some products were no longer supported – and we needed to decide how to approach pages for that.

Within eight months, this organising had paid off. We quadrupled the amount of traffic and made the site faster by removing legacy pages and organising the metadata with clearer intent and purpose. For example, we had more than 300 documents labelled 'installation guide' and we needed to change them to 'Red Hat Enterprise Linux Installation Guide' and so forth.

I was the border collie of all of our content, herding it into little groups and putting it in the pens, but the results were fantastic. I got rid of more content than we generated because I was able to organise it in a way that created a higher individual value for each page.

We are making progress with findability, but I wouldn't want to suggest that everybody's finding what they're looking for and my work here is done. I can always do better. And I'm not popping any champagne corks over a 1 per cent increase.

If I were to boil down everything that I've just talked about into actionable advice, I'd start with this:

- Firstly, understand what humans want to accomplish or aquire on your site.
- Improve your site technology and architecture to improve 'crawlability' by search engines.
- Monitor your site-search data as you would data from Google.
- Improve your speed and core web vitals, not because Google says so, but because it's a good user experience that helps SEO with the ultimate goal of conversions.
- Build content that is supportive of topics and the needs of your users.
- Support your content with ontologies, taxonomies, metadata and schema.
- Make strategic changes to content to support topical relevancy and the keyword-intent data captured from search engines.
- Continually improve your platform and architecture (both information and technical), and connect your content and product pages to conversion data from site search.

DOES SEARCH HAVE A FUTURE?

As a behaviour, search is only going to get bigger. Why? Because we are going to have more things to search upon. Game consoles have search features, phones have search features, Netflix has a search feature. As the number of platforms we use every day increases, search, as a behaviour, is increasing.

Will we still have SEO? That really depends on how search engines, and search, evolves.

I think that SEO in 10 years is going to look very, very different. That's why I'm really focusing on the concept of findability now.

Findability is about taking a more holistic view of search as a tactic, of chat as a tactic, of search platforms as a tactic. I think people will try to automate search through AI, but I think that they will have limited success.

There will be parts of things that can be assisted by AI, and I already use supervised machine learning to predict intent through my own site search.

Ultimately, using AI or machine learning as an assisted technology will create better results for search. But it's not a replacement for people.

I'm very sceptical about having AI or machine learning as a replacement for human insight into fellow humans' intent and ingenuity.

USING AGILE TO SCALE SEO ACROSS A FTSE 100 BUSINESS

JACK SPERRY

SEO DIRECTOR, PHOTOBOX

Jack has been managing teams and developing talent at mobile operator EE since 2016.

He is an SEO leader with a decade of experience working in environments from FTSE 100 companies to startup ventures.

He is currently responsible for all in-house SEO at BT, across the BT, EE and PlusNet brands, helping drive triple-digit year-on-year growth in these key trading areas.

At time of interview Jack was SEO Manager at BT

We talk a lot about how the number one job for SEO today is to connect with the business so you understand what the brand does and what its customers want.

I absolutely agree with that, but I also know that it can be hard, because there is a lot on your typical SEO's plate right now.

I prefer to say, 'what can we really be sure about, in SEO?'.

We know that what's important to the business is what drives value to the business – and that's its customers.

I think one of the things that I've been very successful at doing during my career is making sure that SEO is delivering things that drive value. If we're not building content around what people search for – we need to be.

This tends to centre on getting the basics right, and also following best practice from Google.

We need to always strip it right down to the roots and ask, 'why are we doing that?'. And if we're not providing value, that's a big problem.

With a major business as complex as BT, you're typically looking at months, or perhaps years, for something to be implemented that moves the needle.

I soon realised that, if we wanted to make SEO matter, we had to get much, much more efficient with our time, and to get things into the business quicker.

Always thinking in the long-term meant we had great long-term SEO plans, but these were often invalidated by a change in the wider business. Our ideas were constantly failing to be implemented.

So my problem was clear – how can I make SEO delivery more efficient here?

BEING MORE AGILE TO BUILD BETTER RELATIONSHIPS

We needed something new, because the traditional method of delivering SEO recommendations wasn't really working.

We needed to increase the speed at which we delivered our SEO recommendations. So what we've done is to make SEO at BT into an 'agile' process.

If you're not familiar with agile, it's a really effective project-management approach that came out of software development.

We started with some very early experiments, and have been building and iterating our ways of working ever since.

That in itself is very true to the agile philosophy. It handles change very well too – and in a very complex enterprise organisation such as BT – change can really make or break projects.

Being able to respond to change better seemed like something we should be exploring and soon after adopting agile, we became very comfortable with change. Now we fully embrace and welcome it.

To handle change at this scale and frequency, we break down all of our bigger pieces of work into smaller, less complex pieces. We also ensure requests are very easy to understand. And the good news is – instead of having a spiky shape of delivery – we now have a smoother, more consistent pipeline that's easier for other teams to implement.

That has helped us, because we can now understand the impact of any changes, then scale what worked across other parts of the business to replicate the same thing. That's really useful.

And as we started to work in a more agile way, we also shifted our SEO to-do list from personal or team notebooks, and Outlook and Excel files, into an interactive, real-time board. This means anyone in the business can see what we're working on.

There's a definite, virtuous circle here – by becoming more transparent – the level of buy-in and engagement from our stakeholders has improved, because they have greater visibility of what we're doing.

And this matters, because we can't build relationships with everyone in the business – there's just too many people. So we have to be super-transparent, super-upfront and make everything we're doing is digestible, to any team, no matter what its shape or size.

RIP IT UP AND START AGAIN

We effectively ripped up the traditional SEO way of doing things and rebuilt it all from scratch, based around the agile methodology, and it's been quite exciting.

Would agile suit everybody? I don't know that you can lift and shift the entire model, but I think you should definitely cherry-pick certain elements.

For example, one thing that we do every month is have what we call a 'retrospective'. This is where everyone in the team comes together, and we talk about what went well, what didn't, what we think we need to improve and so on.

It's a safe space to learn from the month or the 'sprint' (an agile term for a period of work) that's just gone. Our analysis continues to grow of our work and we iterate based on what we're learning, and I think that's something people could do elsewhere.

It honestly doesn't matter if you're a team of two people or 10, in any organisation. If you take the time to reflect on what's working well and what isn't working, and are looking to improve over a consistent period, this is something that any SEO, or SEO team can do.

Finally, I think it's a very fair question to ask if all this has worked commercially, as BT's mission is always to make more money and get more traffic.

That happens to be a nice question to answer. In my first week, after I had done all the internal training and induction, I sat down in my first real meeting...

Every Thursday, the analytics team used to send this big pack of trade performance data, and in that first meeting, on the third or fourth slide, it said SEO traffic was down 40 percent on the year. I remember everyone just looking at me and it was very clear that my new mission was to try to improve that.

Since that meeting, we were up double digits at the end of the year, albeit not by a great deal. Every year subsequently, I delivered consistent, year-over-year growth, which I'm quite proud of, and which is quite hard to do in our space.

The mission now is to carry on, and get more traffic, solve more customer queries and earn more money. And it's one I am delighted to have taken on, and which we are now doing in a much more agile way.

WHO I WANT TO SEE ON MY SEO TEAM

When I think about who I would hire at BT, it really depends on the job requirement.

I build a matrix of what I think we're good at and where we think we need support, and I look for people that either make us better, fill a gap, or who can amplify something we're already quite good at. That really depends on the shape of the team at that point in time.

I also think about the direction I think the business is going in, as well as the industry itself, to make sure we build-in some longevity. I'm aware that sounds like a typical SEO response – 'it depends!' – but generally speaking, I have to prioritise filling gaps or making the overall team better when it comes to recruitment.

There may be some innate personal qualities that make a good SEO. A pervading trait we tend to see across the industry, and it has great value, is natural curiosity. The reason this is so important is that, when you strip away all of the fancy terminology around SEO, and all of the whitepapers and blog posts and tools, all you're really doing is lifting the hood up on a website, having a look at how it works and suggesting improvements.

So you also need to like going into detail, finding ways to tinker and making things better. You don't find many SEOs who are builders – if we were thinking about an F1 car – SEOs wouldn't be designing it, they're the people saying later, 'if you just change those wheels a little bit, you'll go a little bit faster'. It's perhaps not the most exciting career, creatively, if you compare it to like design, or even copywriting, or paid media. We spend a lot of time looking at code and spreadsheets and data, and making small changes, and you have to be okay with that from the start.

You also need the ability to pivot very quickly into different ways of thinking and working. That's a very handy attribute for an SEO, both for an agency and in-house in bigger organisations. Beyond that, people come into SEO from all sorts of amazing backgrounds: technical, content, journalism, marketing or general business.

If you want to know how to build a great career for yourself in SEO, the advice I would give to anyone is, first and foremost, to read and learn as much as possible. You also need to look to apply those learnings as quickly as possible. After all, there's a lot of theory out there, but it's quite hard to remember if you don't use it.

Plus, you must have a website you're building in your spare time, because there are going to be opportunities or ideas that you can't necessarily apply within a work context.

Finally, don't be afraid to get things wrong, be very humble, expect to make mistakes, but always look to learn from them.

BE PREPARED, BE REALISTIC – BUT EXPECT THE UNEXPECTED – WHEN DOING A BIG INFRASTRUCTURE PROJECT IN-HOUSE

JENNI STACEY

HEAD OF WEB EXPERIENCE, THE ACCESS GROUP

Jenni started working in SEO in 2009, armed with a marketing degree.

Over the last decade, she has worked everywhere from B2B financial and professional services, to B2C home furnishings and sports, in large corporations and growing SMEs.

Along the way, she's completed multiple website migrations and CMS replatforms.

All of that experience has come in useful since Jenni took on the challenge of heading up the web team at The Access Group, a major supplier of B2B software.

My story is about joining a new company that's very different to anywhere I'd worked before – and within seven months – securing a budget, and conducting a complete restructure of the information architecture (IA) of its highly complex website.

I didn't win the budget for this project just by saying I was going to improve SEO and bring more traffic to the site. I had to talk about how the work would bring more quality, targeted traffic, which would ultimately lead to more conversions – because we would know what users are searching for, and would be serving information that both search engines and humans understand.

Communicating this – and getting buy-in – is about knowing what's important to the senior stakeholder that you're talking to. You have to understand the metrics the business is measuring success on and know the specific benefit you're going to bring, in their areas of the business.

I had the figures showing the volumes we were getting through organic traffic and how the conversion rate was 'only X percent, and how that means there is Y opportunity because we could be converting so many more people'.

I had found where the gaps were, I also knew how to plug them – and changing the URLs for pages on the website could make a big impact.

But I had to be on top of my game.

Many months of hard graft later and we're in an objectively better position. Once the work had been done, the site saw a 20 percent increase in organic traffic.

In the spirit of best practice and sharing useful insights within the SEO community, values I hold dear, I'm going to try to offer some practical learnings on this that I hope others will find useful.

TRANSFORMING THE IA

The older IA had been created without a strategy, added to over time, and wasn't optimised for SEO. It was difficult for search engines to navigate, understand and prioritise our content for SERPs.

In sharp contrast, the new IA was planned and created using a data-led approach, with SEO at the forefront. As a result, we now have a scalable framework that will be able to support business growth.

There was a lot of heavy lifting involved in creating this. I hired an agency to help with the intensive data crunching, which I knew I needed to inform and shape the new framework and URL mapping.

That meant 27,000 keywords were analysed, prioritised and assigned to over 2,000 target pages. In addition, my team and I moved, and rebuilt pages, in their new locations in the CMS and put hundreds of 301 redirects in place.

The reason I suggested the IA project was my conviction that good SEO comes as part of a coherent whole. In my current role, my remit covers all the fun acronyms, like UX and design, CRO, SEO, content and development. While they all have the ability to stand alone, they're intrinsically linked, and they all do a much better job when they work together, sharing knowledge and building on each other.

What my senior leaders found out when I was interviewing for the role was that I'd already had a good long look at the website and it was a bit of a mess.

There was no scalable URL strategy. Sections had been bolted on as the business had grown, so the keywords used in the URLs were all over the place, and there was a lot of duplicate content.

At the interview, I may have slightly surprised them by saying that job number one had to be sorting that out. I also pointed out that because Access is continuing to grow, we would need an architecture to support that, so there'd be clear pathways for expansion.

A TRUE AGENCY AND IN-HOUSE PARTNERSHIP

I needed to get all my data in line first, to do the job right. That's why I found an agency's help so useful. Because we have complex products and solutions, in many industries, sorting out all the keywords and pages was a big task.

It was very collaborative, because, as the agency gave us that data, we as the in-house team could put the business context around it. My team is brilliant and I am very pro in-house, but there are limitations, in terms of SEO resources.

With an in-house team, SEO is most likely just one of many things that you look after, so bringing in an external resource to help you when appropriate is something that no good in-house SEO should have a problem with. Why not get someone in who's an expert and does SEO day in, day out?

At the same time, it's all about finding an external partner who can act as an extension of your team. They need to embrace your culture and you need to embrace theirs.

I find that if you are really transparent with each other and foster a culture of honesty, great results can happen. Your agency has to be able to say when something isn't achievable – whether it's the timescales or scope of work. That openness helps you both, in turn.

I also find, if I'm absolutely clear with my external partners about the scope and what I expect, they find it much easier to work to the brief. Also – no question is a silly question.

GETTING THE RIGHT TOOLS

As well as knowing when to call on external help, there are some tools that are a great help in our work.

Google Data Studio is an incredibly important tool for creating dashboards to monitor performance and progress – I use it every day.

Screaming Frog is always helpful – and it's really inexpensive. It crawls the entire website and tells you all sorts of information about each page. It will pull out the URL, the metadata, the titles, descriptions, and then you can pull it into a big spreadsheet. For the IA, I used it to draw down all of the URLs I needed to move from one place to another, then mapped them to their new locations.

Google Sheets is great, but there are some things that you can't do in it – Excel is, of course, another major SEO tool and knowing how to do a VLOOKUP is a life-changing skill. The Office365 capability to work in the same document together is really helpful now.

Semrush, Google Analytics and Google Search Console were all very useful to draw down search impressions, clicks and volumes too.

WHAT WE'VE LEARNED... SO FAR

In every CMS I've ever worked on, there are different quirks, so my advice is to take the time to plan it out properly. Break it down by page, or section, but try to figure out how long you actually need and be clear that it's going to be a repetitive task.

If it takes half an hour to rebuild a page and move it, then times that by how many pages you've got – and your timings might end up being realistic. I had every single member of my team, including myself, doing what needed to be done to move the pages from one location to another, and it was a massive job.

The next job was a new navigation for an improved UX and best-practice signposting for search engines, which is now out in the wild and already showing improvements in conversations.

Then there's the consolidation of our content, which has started with the blog, and is another lovely SEO tidying-up task. We had approximately 2,000 blogs at the start of this process, to give you an idea of scale. Again, there was a lot of repetitive content accrued over the years.

We used Screaming Frog to draw down all the posts, then cross-referenced this with data from tools like Semrush, Google Search Console and Google Analytics to tell us how each of those blogs was performing. This is the kind of task where VLOOKUPs come in very handy!

We're being very cut-throat. If it's over a year old and it's got under a certain number of views and under a certain amount of search equity, then it's gone, because it's just wasting our crawl budget. If there's any content in there that can be amalgamated, let's do that.

Why is this review and consolidation important? Let's say a reader is searching for, 'what is absence management software?'. The reader's intent is to find information, they want to know something, but they're not ready to buy yet. That's where a blog comes in.

If we have that keyword peppered throughout five different blogs though – how does Google know which of those to serve to that reader? We were diluting our equity, so it's better to optimise and frequently update one blog, rather than having several that talk about the same thing.

We overran on the first phase – really, because we're in-house, we know SEO is just one of the things that we do – so when other priority projects come in, or a pandemic hits, then your timelines take a hit.

You need to be agile and move with it. Be prepared for the unexpected – in other words – something always disrupts your timelines.

We're on a journey and there's still a lot of work to be done but, this is amazing, rewarding work and I am getting so much satisfaction making real, positive change here.

WHY – AND HOW – TO GET THE BEST OUT OF YOUR DEVELOPERS

ROXANA STINGU

HEAD OF SEO, ALAMY

After a decade helping the hosting industry with its SEO, including working for major brands like GoDaddy, Roxana made a career change two years ago to work for stock photography agency Alamy.

She is all about sharing best practice within the SEO community – so others can get to the same conclusions she did, but faster.

Roxana is a technical specialist – but her focus for Mastering In-house SEO this year is a people issue – how to work best with developers.

Alamy was my first and only interview in 10 years – and I realised very quickly that it would be a very different SEO job to what I had done before.

I used to work as part of the marketing team and would get access to development resources sporadically. Now I sit under product – and, as a result – get to work with development on a daily basis. And so I now have a lot more insight into how hard developers work.

I used to think I had a very good handle on how to get things done without continuous access to developers. But the past couple of years have taught me just how much more I can achieve when I do have their ongoing support.

I'm part of many online SEO communities and I see that many technical SEOs are unhappy with how developers react to their requests.

A common theme relates to the SEO putting together a 32-page audit, which the developers have not addressed, even months later. And there's far too much advice out there that says all you need to do is 'bribe' them to get them to like you. 'Just buy them pizza and beer!'.

If any of this sounds familiar, after two years in this role, I can now shed some light on what's really going wrong – and explain why it might not be your developers' fault.

THE TRUTH ABOUT DEVELOPERS

At Alamy, our focus is more on image search than web search, and that's something I hadn't properly worked on before.

We have a very big website, with 250 million images live as Mastering In-house SEO goes to press, the equivalent of having 250 million products on any other ecommerce website. I think we can agree that's a lot. And it's also a lot of infrastructure to keep running.

Coming into this role, I was expecting the developers to know about everything I worked with. I quickly found that they didn't and the reason for that is because they just have completely different focus.

All too often, an SEO runs a tool, it comes back with an audit, and they 'copy' and 'paste' that without even thinking about what implementation on the website actually involves. They just send it to a developer, hoping they will know exactly what the results mean, without considering that the SEO tools are written for, well, SEOs.

You're missing the fact that these developers might have spent all their life in the backend and in that case, they don't need to even know basic HTML, even though we think it's simple. Truth be told, if they already knew about SEO, what would be the point of me even being there in the first place?

I used to always be annoyed with the developers I was working with for not seeing the importance of my 'genius' audits. Now, I know another reason why they acted that way was because they work differently to most other departments.

When it comes to development, most companies follow an 'agile' methodology – and although this time frame can be different – a typical implementation of that involves working in two-weeks sprints.

On top of this, future sprints may be planned in advance, so no new items will make their way in unless they're critical to the business, or could lead to a massive revenue increase.

Whatever pattern they're working to, this still means that no developer is going to even look at your audit until their current and any planned sprints are done.

So, we're often asking them to do stuff that requires them to learn something new, before actually tackling a task, which perhaps they didn't really have time to do in the first place.

It's like we are speaking different languages – if they speak French and German all day, and you give them stuff in Italian – they can't learn 'Italian' overnight to fix your problem.

Developers speak different 'languages' in other ways too. Sometimes, they just have a different interaction style.

PUTTING YOUR OWN WORK IN

I would always complain to my manager that our developers weren't implementing redirects properly. But thinking back, I pretty much just gave them a list and said, 'page A needs to redirect to page B', without considering anything in between. So, being very busy people, my developers were implementing exactly what I asked for and all this did was result in 'redirect chains', due to older, already pre-existing rules.

I used to think 'such lazy developers', when the fact is, I was the one that could have prevented this. They didn't have the time, nor was it their responsibility, to go through 2,000 lines of .htaccess file to find dependencies

That's when I realised that I could learn about .htaccess, so I could figure out any dependencies and give the developers the extra changes required to avoid these issues. All I had to do was to ask for a copy of the file.

But, while, you might think you can just learn about something like .htaccess and figure out the dependencies – it doesn't help you with the issue about a lack of time.

Another area where we can make a developer's life easier is page speed. We know that Google is pushing the new Web Core Vitals, rolling out new performance metrics to measure our websites against. They're a bit more complicated than the ones we had before, so there may be SEOs who don't quite get them yet. And developers don't get them either – these metrics are as new for them as they are for anybody else.

There are also new words Google has introduced into our vocabulary – and we all have to learn what they are. If we use these new terms with our developers, without any kind of in-house training, they're going to look at them thinking 'I don't know what these are, and, frankly, I don't have the time to read about them'.

What's much better is for you to put in your own time, do some research into the issues. Rather than giving the developer a generic audit tool report, you can give them actions that are specific to your website. Or, you could reduce your audit 'ask' from 32 pages to a list of 10 quick things they can do, and you're going to make a lot of progress, surprisingly quickly.

SUPPORTING YOUR COLLEAGUES TO SUPPORT YOU

If you decide you want to put in the time to improve the SEO-development relationship, why not:

- Learn to 'speak developer', as it's less of an effort for one person to do this than for whole development teams to learn how to 'speak SEO'. You don't have to become fluent, conversational is enough to get started.
- To do this, you could join daily 'stand-ups' and refinement meetings as an observer to better understand their workflow.
- Or, ask your colleagues for a meeting where they explain what they do in their day-to-day and what tools they use. Ask them what frustrations they get from the way you raise SEO-related issues and how you can make them better.

Then, you could implement an education process by offering to give developers an overview of all the new things Google is pushing, for example, making them aware of the importance of websites being mobile-friendly by explaining the mobile-only index, or explaining how search-engine crawling can make or break a website's visibility and showing them case studies about how improving the efficiency of crawls can lead to massive gains.

When your developers start to understand the importance and impact of your requests, or what happens when they make page changes, suggest they might check the mobile version too and ensure their changes leave the page mobile-friendly. When they create a new page, they might run

LightHouse on it to see how good their work is.

Finally, when they see search-engine crawl rates fluctuate unnaturally, they will know they need to raise it with you too. But if nobody tells them about these things, how can they even start thinking about them?

GETTING THE RESULTS YOU WANT

Even though it might take time, I definitely think it's worth doing. The results we're getting at Alamy show why. When I joined, the organic traffic trend was at 3.4 million – now, it's up to 7.7 million.

None of that SEO success would have been possible before, because 90 percent of the improvements are down to technical work, where my team and the developers worked in lockstep. Most of us don't have access to an SEO-specific developer, so the easier we make it for our colleagues, the better it's going to be for us. And that's how you're going to get what you want done.

And, as a result of all this hard work, I know what success looks like – it's when developers start telling you about SEO. That's when you've taught them enough so that they can let you know what improvements you can make, without you asking. Now, projects are coming out better than I planned only because of developers raising their concerns or sharing their ideas.

And because they're more technical and know the website set-up better than us, they can come up with some of the best ideas that you couldn't even think of.

WHEN I HIRE AN SEO – I'M LOOKING FOR A 'DETECTIVE'

The most important things when recruiting an SEO have to be that they are curious and analytical. You can teach somebody the basic elements of SEO, you can teach them technical stuff, but you can't teach them native traits. I will always trade seniority for potential and hire people who are analytical, curious and passionate about SEO in general, over people who meet the 'years of experience' criteria.

After all, SEO should be fun – isn't it like playing detective all day? I used to read a lot of Agatha Christie, and in a way, I'm a 'detective' in my professional life. What we're doing all day long is sticking our noses everywhere, trying to figure out why things work, or why they don't.

In SEO, you have all these tools that do all the work for you, using machine learning and artificial intelligence, but at the end of the day, you still need a curious person to put the clues together and come up with answers.

SEO IS THE NEW 'PRODUCT'

IGAL STOLPNER

FORMER VP GROWTH & SEO, INVESTING.COM

Investing.com is a global, financial-markets platform available in more than 30 languages.

After being central to the platform's success for the past 13 years, Igal is now seeking new challenges, but staying on as his former department's advisor.

His next move? Consulting on international SEO, while opening his own firm, where he will once again be running in-house SEO.

My biggest professional achievement has been taking Investing.com from zero traffic when we started back in 2007 to being one of the largest 200 sites globally.

That means it gets more than 200 million monthly visits – and we achieved that mainly through SEO and word-of-mouth buzz.

Obviously, we had quite a few challenges in the early days. From deciding at launch that we needed to be available in multiple languages, to consolidating domains, to later adding complementary apps that drove a massive part of our focus and resources.

Back then, to succeed in SEO, the discussion was mainly around three things: creating more content, pointing out its top keywords and building links.

All three are still massive, and still drive many of the efforts being made in SEO today, but the focus has shifted – quality has won over quantity. And tons of other ranking factors that have popped up too.

And to be fair, for the first two years that we were in business – our focus was on these three things. The guy who runs sales could come to me on a Monday morning and say, 'we need more traffic from France or UAE', and I'd shift the focus to these countries and see results the same week.

But things just don't work that way anymore. Our actions now will only impact in weeks, sometimes even in months.

With all of these other ranking factors in mind, the link profile of a site remains very important. But there are two things to keep in mind here.

First, the approach to this is now totally different, and in-house SEOs won't be taking unnecessary risks for their companies anymore.

Second, for many in-house SEO teams, we're speaking about quite well-known brands. And when we're speaking about running the SEO of a strong online brand, getting new links becomes secondary because these are simply coming naturally.

So what's more important is to direct people to the right place, which means more work on internal architecture, greater focus on content, site features and overall experience.

In short, for many in-house SEO teams today, links are important, especially monitoring them well, but getting them is no longer a big part of the day-to-day.

After 13 years working in-house, and seeing how the SEO world has changed since 2007, I want to share some of the most useful things I've learned about becoming an in-house SEO leader.

SEOS NEED TO BE UNDERSTOOD

If you want to be a successful in-house SEO, then you must be integrated into the company's processes.

What that looks like might be different from one company to another, because companies are all structured in different ways, and they may all understand 'marketing' differently.

For some companies, marketing means 'performance marketing' before anything else. For others, marketing first of all means 'branding'. And there are some that simply refer to 'marketing' as to 'the funnel of acquiring users' – the whole thing, from A to Z.

SEO is also positioned differently between one firm to another, some see it as a 'marketing channel', while others see it as a more 'product-integrated' component.

Despite these differences, all businesses need to answer the same core questions – 'what is it we want to achieve? Where do we want to be in a year? Is SEO the right channel for us to focus on? Do we have what it takes to allow SEO to be successful for us? What personnel do we need?' and many more besides.

So how can you become integrated in your company's processes?

My advice is to make sure that you are heard. That means making sure people understand the complexity of SEO – and the impact that business decisions can have on SEO in the long run. It sounds easy, but in most cases, it's not. In fact, as an SEO leader, a huge part of your job is being SEO's public-relations person.

Too often companies don't involve the SEO team until long after a decision has been made. This means the product, the page, the category is already specified, sometimes already up to UX and design. Then, they want your team to 'SEO it', a ridiculous thing to even say. In 2021, you can't 'SEO something' unless you're part of the fundamentals.

You want to make sure that the investment is clear to your company's management – and that making SEO part of the product-development process is a critical factor.

And nothing critical for SEO should not be ignored simply because someone thinks it's small – including tags – which are often referred to as something that will be 'handled' later.

The alternative is constantly fixing things that could be built better in the first place, and becoming a constant roadblock to the company's processes. Nobody wants to be the one who makes things stuck.

IN-HOUSE, WE DON'T SPEAK ENOUGH ABOUT MONEY

Realistically, we can't become a part of the product unless we clearly map out the value of SEO to the business.

A brand running a team of 10 or 20 SEOs in-house is spending quite a lot on an annual basis – and not only on salaries. It's important not just to show positive ROI of our specific actions, but also show clearly how SEO adds value to the business over time.

One of the most important things an in-house SEO can do is make sure there's a clear attribution model. If SEO has driven $300,000 in revenue, whether it's sales or ads, you want to make sure the company is able to track and see it.

Without this sort of information, it's going to be very hard to attract management support – whether that's to bring in new people, source new tools or prioritise development.

As in-house SEOs, often we don't talk enough about money. We all understand that's how the world works, but we need to connect our goals, tactics and actions to the big business goals. Speak the language of who you need on your side.

THE PRACTICAL TOOLS THAT 'AGILE' CAN GIVE YOUR TEAM

About seven years ago, I was introduced to 'agile' methodology. And it has really changed the way I work as an SEO, from using Kanban for managing my own and my team's tasks, to how to manage meetings, to how to handle a backlog of tasks, specifically when it comes to 'waiting for dev' tasks.

Every Monday, I start planning the week ahead, but I also start each day by checking in on the status of everything – and prioritise accordingly.

The Kanban board truly helps you visualise your status and spot things that are stuck for any reason. It also helps you pivot if you've been stuck with something for a while and get back to it later with a fresh mind.

'Stand-up' meetings let you check-in on your team, and their tasks, on a daily basis and help them solve issues that are very often smaller than you or they might think.

One of the issues with handling the backlog of tasks is that many things are dependent on third-party resources, from design to content, from product specs to dev. As a result, these things often frustrate the team, especially those younger folks who come into SEO with lots of energy.

I find young, smart, technical SEOs have an idea they want to push – and it's difficult when the manager tells them 'okay, but we have to wait for weeks now because dev has more important things to handle'. While waiting may be alright as there are other priorities, what's important as an in-house SEO is to be able to move on to the next thing easily.

Agile helps you manage a backlog of tasks in a way that you can jump between those that require third-party resources and those that don't. This balance can be crucial for the team's wellbeing.

One of the other agile principles that I think is extremely valuable for in-house SEOs is having a 'fast lane' for the things that matter the most. It's something that's easy to take advantage of, but when managed correctly, you should only use it for items that are crucial.

Using it in this way means that I can go to the CTO and get the resources of a developer immediately, whether that's to solve a rendering problem or attack a new opportunity.

Without this system in place, the danger is that you spot an opportunity, but you have to sit and wait for four weeks. By the time we get there, it might not be relevant.

As an in-house SEO leader, you are often going to find yourself stuck between your company's management and your team. Agile principles will help you spot the crucial things, and never completely abandon the less-urgent, yet still-important things, and help you constantly push your team forward.

ARE 'PRODUCT SUGGESTIONS' THE NEW 'CONTENT CREATION' THAT SEO NEEDS?

About five years ago, I stumbled on a keyword that we weren't ranking for at all, 'trending stocks'. Well, the truth is that we simply didn't have a page for it.

At this point, we already had tons of user data on both the web and apps. And usually, we'd use data for stories, PR and link building, but not site features.

Then I realised that most of the results ranking for this term were pages showing stocks that were trending over the past few weeks or months – for a market that is changing sometimes daily. As a stock investor, I want to see stocks that are trending now.

So the team decided to build a page that shows trending stocks in real-time, based on what users are searching for. New stocks would get more weight, popular stocks less, and with the volume of data, we had enough information to build a real-time index.

The magic worked, users loved it, and with absolutely no external link-building efforts, this page ranked number one, within less than four months from launch, for a competitive keyword. Now five years later – it's still stable between positions one to three.

SEO doesn't replace product management, but since everyone's searching on Google all the time and there's such a shift to quality and expertise in the SERPs, it only makes sense for SEOs to think 'as product'. Why not push feature suggestions just as much as we used to think about creating content?

What's great about being an in-house SEO is the substantial focus you can have. You are the true expert, the one who understands the site and industry around it better than anyone else at your firm.

It allows you to monitor things closely, and watch your competitors as a detective.

Making sure your needs are clear to other stakeholders and senior management is crucial, and a big part of your job is both making sure that you're understood, and that your team is never left behind.

Since we don't live in a perfect world, and things can be pivoted and delayed, agile principles offer a few fantastic tactics for SEOs. Lastly, think as a product manager – every page is a landing page – and you will only rank better when your site offers a better alternative. So be the best product.

KEEP YOUR EYE ON WHERE THE BALL'S GOING – BUT IMPLEMENT WHAT'S WORKING RIGHT NOW

STEVEN VAN VESSUM

VP OF COMMUNITY, CONTENTKING

Doing SEO since 2007 and 'still in love with it', Steven has progressed from a number of digital-marketing and SEO roles into co-founding a real-time SEO auditing and content change-tracking platform, ContentKing.

As a result, he and his team have unique insight into the most

Sometimes SEO can just seem really hard. It's so competitive out there.

But any SEO can make a difference, as long as they pick a good battleground to start their 'war' with the competition. You need to have faith that if your users love visiting your website, they're bound to come back whenever a new question arises.

Whatever else it is, SEO is about trying to remove as much uncertainty as possible so you can really focus on the things that matter.

If you have good SEO processes, monitoring software in place – so you don't have to worry about unexpected SEO surprises – and you're always looking at the bigger picture, you're going to do fine.

Even if you're a small player and don't have much authority in the market when you start, it's easy to earn a reputation by working on site authority and trust, building links and continually providing value in the content you create.

One idea is to pick a topic that wouldn't make sense for some of your larger competitors to write about because of its relatively low search volume. That's a quick win to start with, and once you make a couple of those, you may be able to take on some of your competitors with more competitive topics.

By being smart about the battles you fight, you can quickly build up reputation and traffic.

RE-INVESTING IN THE BASICS

What's surprising to me, and also really refreshing, is how much impact you can have by getting the basics right.

The way we started doing content marketing and SEO was by constantly producing new articles, but the ROI from those was pretty low. They weren't ranking on the first page of Google – we just weren't getting a lot of organic traffic.

In response, towards the end of 2019, we started running some experiments. Rather than focusing on producing new content, we made some updates to existing content.

The ROI on the initial investment increased massively with just a couple of hours of updating, which only really involved some restructuring and updating with new relevant information, tweaking the internal-link structure and re-promoting them.

An article that may have taken two or three days to put together, which hadn't really driven ROI, was now being turned around just by spending four hours updating it. That was a real eye-opener, as it enabled us to significantly increase the return we were getting from work we had already done.

We did this work for around 10 or 15 articles, and the most successful ones doubled or tripled in organic traffic.

The learning here is to always keep your eyes on the prize as an in-house SEO. Don't let new, shiny things distract you – like a magpie.

As an SEO, you know all of the new stuff happening, Google's announcements around things like Page Experience, or the new structured-data types it's releasing.

It's all interesting, of course – and as an SEO professional – you have to know what's going on, and what things like this can and can't do.

But it's easy to get distracted, while, in reality, the more basic stuff is what's driving traffic and making money – and what's messing up traffic and revenue – is (accidentally) getting the basics wrong.

Yet, I still think a lot of people aren't seeing this.

They don't see the value in updating existing content. That may be because management is pushing them to create new stuff, because that feels like you're creating something, which has to lead to more organic traffic.

But in a lot of cases, that's just not true. I would estimate that 95 percent of content that's being published doesn't really get much more than 10 visitors a month.

If you look at your target audience, the issues they're struggling with, and create content that helps them solve their issues, always circling back to a content-led approach, that's what's going to raise your game.

At the same time, if you look at content that performs well, it's usually high-quality content that people learn from and so contains a lot of value. If you're able to create that kind of content, you'll see that other people start linking to it, without you having to ask them.

There's also the SEO best-practice things, like, how you structure your article, how the site content is linked together, linking out to relevant articles and using structured data.

NOT GETTING HUNG UP ABOUT GOOGLE

This is why I don't worry too much about Google. Big Google algorithm updates happen three or four times a year, and a lot of SEO people freak out.

But if you've been paying attention, you know what the algorithms will touch on. And if you've been keeping a clean house, there's nothing to worry about, in most cases.

When I see new Google algorithm update announcements, I take a note and schedule them for the future, to see where to fit it into our content-marketing roadmap, or if we'll need to make changes to our site. But for me, it's about keeping your eyes on where the ball is going, while implementing what's working right now.

A lot of SEOs don't really do that and I think that's a shame, because the stuff that's working right now, is driving results right now.

A lot of businesses, especially during Covid, could really benefit from those good results. It's important to see and understand what's coming down the road, and what kind of impact it may have on the way you work, and the way you do SEO. But it also makes a lot of sense to focus on the here and now, not just the next new things coming to the market.

The chances of a Google update significantly affecting your search results in a negative way is quite low, while the chances of a website update significantly affecting your results in a negative way are high. I don't worry about Google algorithm updates – and I don't think you should – either. Worry about getting, and keeping, all of the basics right.

Do this and your own ROI will increase as an SEO, giving you the confidence to pick a great new battle. Then you can go out and win that one, too.

A DAY IN THE 'SEO LIFE'

I would say that I qualify as an in-house SEO. I don't work for an agency. I'm not a freelancer or an affiliate. And I spend 80 percent of my time on content marketing and SEO. I'm in the trenches myself quite a lot.

The value proposition of ContentKing is about preventing nasty SEO surprises from affecting your bottom line. As soon as something bad happens – something like your robots.txt file being carried over from a test to a production environment – you're notified by us.

You'll know that's bad news, because the production environment needs to be accessible for search engines, and they need to be able to pick up all the new content you're pushing.

That's one of the most common SEO issues we find, and we help both in-house and agency side, but you can't fix things without actually knowing what's going on.

My job goes beyond just SEO, though. As VP of Community, I need to keep in touch with the global SEO and digital-marketing community, making sure people notice our content and product.

It's also about promoting content as well. That means making sure it performs well on social media, among other things. I do a lot of writing and researching, and spend time discussing SEO topics with our team.

At the end of the day, I'm responsible for making sure people come to our website, and if they like what they see, hopefully they'll create a trial account for our software. If that provides value for them, they may sign up and become a customer.

I'm responsible for the first part of that journey. That means driving as much traffic to the site as possible – and enticing visitors to take the free trial. I need to meet that KPI.

From this perspective, I would say SEO goes hand in hand with content marketing, just like proper content writing and promotion.

What's great about my role is that I get to combine SEO with content marketing and PR – and that's a very cool combination of specialties.

SHOULD SEOS ONLY BE OPTIMISING FOR GOOGLE?

I keep an eye on how other search platforms are doing.

DuckDuckGo is growing pretty fast, I admit. But, on the grand scheme of things, they're an ant compared to the elephant, Google.

I don't think it's smart to put all your eggs in one basket, and we do try to diversify our traffic sources to our own site, but at the end of the day, Google's driving the majority for us, and that goes for a lot of other companies too.

At the end of the day, you have to ask yourself, 'if I do get hit by one of the Google updates, will I have trouble operating my business? Will I get into trouble if it takes too long to recover?'.

You should never be in the position where that's the case, so it's a balancing act. It's a case of making sure that your target audience is able to find you – and Google needs to be a big part of that mix – because it's so dominant.

That said, it still makes sense to invest in PPC. Things like Google AdWords, Facebook, LinkedIn – you name it, you should be there.

And don't forget the organic side of things. If you're really into content marketing, you should be spending 50 percent of your time writing content and 50 percent of your time promoting it, so people actually read it. That's where social media comes in.

Ultimately, you need to figure out where your target audience is – and you need to be present. For us, LinkedIn, Twitter and Facebook are definitely interesting, but not so much Pinterest or TikTok.

The only worry I have with all of these options is that there is just not enough competition for Google.

HOW COMBINING DATA, TECHNOLOGY, CONTENT AND PR HELPED HOMETOGO NAVIGATE COVID-19

FELIX WELCKENBACH

DIRECTOR INBOUND MARKETING, HOMETOGO

Felix has more than a decade of international marketing expertise focussed on growing digital businesses.

He started his SEO journey working at online-dating site ParshipMeetGroup before progressing to senior roles at live-entertainment company Eventim and then travel brand Expedia.

He's been in-house, worked as a consultant and currently works at Berlin-based travel firm HomeToGo.

At HomeToGo, it's my job to think about how best to grow organic traffic for our different travel brands and local markets.

The good news is, by adopting a modern and integrated SEO approach, which combines data, technology, content, PR and user experience work, we've created genuine commercial success.

Plus, we've built a reputation as a reliable partner to media companies by providing them with relevant travel data. And this has created a 'flywheel' effect, which has driven further SEO success, all done by our award-winning, in-house team.

USING DATA TO NAVIGATE COVID-19

Obviously, the Covid-19 pandemic has been a very rocky time for the travel industry.

But after the first stage of lockdown, when people were ready to travel again, we noticed that they wanted to avoid hotels, in favour of rural travel, and were travelling mostly domestically.

We were well-positioned to meet this need in terms of vacation inventory, so we started making continuous investments into a better product and user experience – and of course, content – given we knew there would be bigger demand for rental experiences.

We used data-led insights to brush up our landing pages and built back trust with customers by adding things like 'free cancellation' messaging to on-site elements, in order to boost conversion. But it was data-led content that was a big part of our success.

We gave relevant data about travel-behaviour changes to journalists. This helped them navigate their readers (our customers!) through the uncertainty – and inspired the public with ideas about where to go – even down to what prices to expect during the busy summer period. Very quickly, the topic of vacation rentals became mainstream, and was covered in most major media outlets, from Forbes to The Wall Street Journal and The New York Times.

We then continuously provided great data and analysis to our customers about the most in-demand travel destinations, so they could make better-informed decisions. And this in turn drove coverage that really helped to push vacation rentals as an industry, and HomeToGo's brand awareness, domain authority and visibility, in particular.

In the summer months, we saw high-double-digit-growth rates, which in the depths of a global pandemic was quite remarkable. Indeed, a true V-shaped recovery.

Part of that success was driven by a surge in demand for vacation-rental experiences. But, we also saw an increase in rankings and overall visibility, supported by higher conversion rates.

WORKING HARD TO KNOW WHAT WORKS

We work with both internal and external data sources to identify short- and long-term trends. We slice down into different geographies, identifying things like whether people are travelling more domestically, or people are booking further out or closer to the date, and so on.

We've built a process here – working to identify the hottest topics in our markets – and then working with B2B and B2C media to tell compelling stories about them. And I think we are very good at figuring out what and when different stories will be in demand with the media and customers.

We also make sure we use any insights for our own on-site optimisation, creating maximum SEO impact in return. We call this a 'performance-driven' approach to SEO and PR, combining state-of-the-art storytelling with solid on-site work based on a strong technology platform.

Of course, data insights gained from this process really matter to us – but prioritising our tech initiatives and making sure we're easily able to separate important from unimportant tasks – is even more vital.

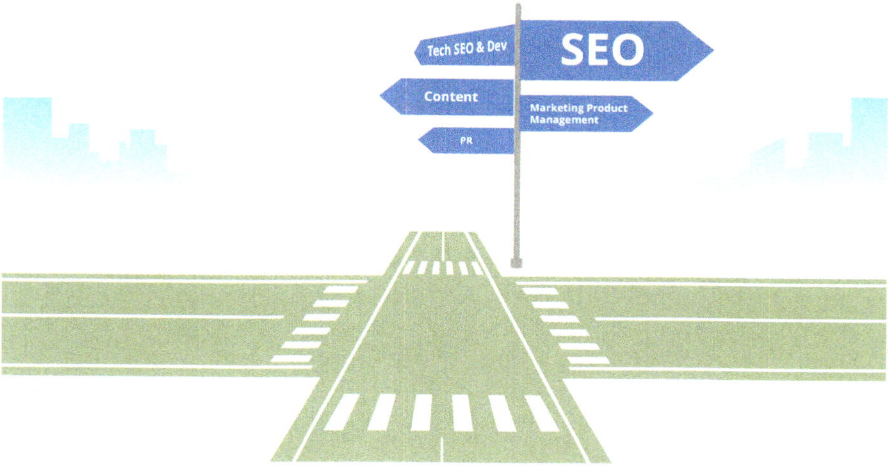

In the end it's all about execution – and it cannot be stressed enough – the importance of having a solid tech foundation that allows the teams to work efficiently and autonomously.

We all have seen the diminishing space for organic traffic that Google gives us (given all the SERP layout changes, more ads and more zero-click searches). For sure, Google is the most important organic traffic source for many businesses, and it has not become easier to acquire customers organically, but hey – there's always market share to gain from your competitors. On top of that, there are alternative organic traffic sources to reach your customers.

Our integrative approach requires commitment. That even means working outside of regular office hours so we're always available to journalists and can deliver on ad hoc demands that come our way.

So yes, hard work – but hard work that means we are achieving a really deep level of trust with the media. Going this extra mile really paid off with that busy summer 2020 period.

THREE KEY THINGS TO GET RIGHT

KNOW YOUR DATA

You don't have to be data analysts as SEOs – but you should be able to find and work with the data you need. Data will help you prioritise your tasks, as well as lead to better informed and quicker decision-making.

Think of it as the 'fuel' you need to power your work. And everyone on the team should have the ability to find the answer to their questions in data. Knowledge of SQL can come in handy here too.

AUTOMATE WHAT YOU CAN

A lot of tasks we perform in SEO are still quite manual and can take up a significant amount of your team's time. Excel and Google Docs are great, but in the case of large-scale datasets, or repetitive analyses, it can get quite messy. So other solutions are likely to be more efficient.

Not every SEO has to be an automation expert or a 'Python ninja', but it's helpful to eliminate these time-consuming tasks by either taking a crack at solving it yourself, having the knowledge on the team, or putting together some technical requirements for a development team to help you.

MAKE SURE YOU'RE MAKING IMPACT

Having sound business judgment is crucial for every SEO – so always make sure you're working on the big-impact areas for the company.

Whether it's working on the product-side improving conversion rates and UX, or working on on-site content and domain authority, be clear on what your strategic goals are, that those fit in with the business and that they are impactful enough.

I've seen teams that are busy working, but they're not generating much output. It's important to ensure you've identified areas of high leverage, to then generate measurable output for the business.

Here, a multifunctional team gives you the ability to move really fast, as long as everyone is incentivised by the same set of objectives.

BEST PRACTICE IS NOT GOING TO GET YOU VERY FAR

SEOs really strive to be very best-practice driven, but it's likely not giving you the returns that you are hoping for. The fact that a set of initiatives works for your competition does not mean it's going to work for you. In fact, it might not move the needle as much as you think.

Instead of just applying all the best-practice basics you've read about – you need to be thinking more strategically about what you want to achieve in the context of your competitive environment. Identify a clear roadmap and set of goals that help you get there – what do you do next to get closer to that goal?

Relentlessly test your hypotheses – find out what works for you and your brand and what does not. And – most importantly of all – don't follow everything everyone else is doing – execute, measure, adjust, then repeat.

STRATEGY IN ACTION – HOW AUTOTRADER BROUGHT THE 'SMELL OF SUCCESS' INTO OUR BID TO BOOST SALES OF NEW CARS

ADAM WHITTLES

HEAD OF SEO, AUTOTRADER

Adam has more than 10 years of experience in digital marketing and is currently Head of SEO at AutoTrader, the UK's largest automotive marketplace.

As part of the marketing leadership team, Adam is jointly responsible for the company's marketing budget, objectives and strategy, as well as managing the SEO team.

He has previously held roles at a number of WPP/GroupM media agencies, including Head of SEO and Content Marketing at Mindshare.

Before joining AutoTrader, he managed the SEO programme for Apple across EMEIA and emerging markets.

When I joined AutoTrader in the summer of 2019, one of the first things I had to do was figure out how SEO could make the most impact.

Of course, there were (and still are) a number of technical issues that need to be worked through, but I quickly spotted an opportunity with our digital PR and brand-marketing team. Not long before I joined, the brand-marketing team had hired an exceptional campaign manager who had already achieved success with a number of PR campaigns and stunts.

Having already championed the value of digital PR for earning quality links back to the website, we set to work on a collaboration for an ambitious campaign...

MAKING SCENTS OF THE CAMPAIGN

AutoTrader is a familiar brand to most people, many of whom have fond memories of flipping through our magazines looking at the variety of cars on offer.

We're very well known as a marketplace for used cars, but perhaps not so much for selling new cars, even though this has been a major focus for the business for quite some time. While our brand awareness for new cars has steadily increased over the years, there's still room to grow further.

For SEO specifically, we track a number of 'new car' related searches – many of which we perform well for, but there was one term that eluded us – 'new car deals'. As you can imagine, this is a very valuable term to rank for, as it comes with clear commercial intent.

Prior to the campaign, we were floating between page two and page three of Google – essentially invisible to most users – and one of the first key SEO contributions at this point was to find the right agency to work with.

This may sound like a simple task, but there were many factors that needed to be considered in order for us to find an agency that would satisfy both our brand, and SEO, objectives.

Given that the budget for this sat with the brand team, there needed to be a lot of collaboration between this team and mine to ensure we were both happy. Clear communication and mutual respect were very important here – making it clear why a specific agency was preferred over another.

NOTHING IS MORE MEMORABLE THAN A SMELL...

Once we had selected an agency to work with, the next step was to find a creative idea that related to our 'new car' product. One of the ideas suggested by the agency was to create an AutoTrader fragrance.

Believe it or not, this was not the first time the idea had been suggested by an agency to the brand team. But, with new faces on both the brand and SEO teams, we decided to execute it.

Fortunately, the concept tied-in to some research that AutoTrader had conducted, looking into what the public associated with brand-new cars. Our research showed that brand-new cars were commonly associated with 'success', particularly the smell of a new car. With this in mind, we decided to bottle the 'smell of a new car' and commissioned a perfume supplier to create a limited-edition run of the bespoke fragrance.

WHAT'S IN A NAME?

Every time the idea of an AutoTrader fragrance had been mooted, the same name was always suggested – Eau de Trader.

While this is an amusing play on the brand name of AutoTrader, we felt this would not tie-in well with the business objectives of the campaign – which was about promoting the 'new car' product. Therefore, we pushed for the name Eau de New Car, which we felt would perform much better.

As simple as it may sound, the campaign name can make all the difference. If you can imagine all the press coverage we got for this launch, they all mentioned the 'new car' product we cared about, simply by referencing the fragrance name.

Not only does this help our brand awareness for 'new car', but it also helps to improve our SEO performance and relevance for 'new car' related terms.

SMELLS LIKE NEW CAR SPIRIT

So what did we actually do for the campaign? There were quite a few elements and teams that came together to create this campaign, perhaps more than you might have expected:

- The fragrance – as mentioned, we commissioned a perfume supplier to create the fragrance and the bottle. This was not exactly straightforward and required some back and forth – our design team wasn't happy with the initial labels and quality of the bottle, so quite a few changes had to be made before we were able to make it available to buy.

- The landing page – although the launch of the perfume coincided with April Fools' Day, it was very much a serious product that you could buy, assuming you could afford the £175 price tag. This added new complexity for AutoTrader as we are not an e-commerce business and so it was a challenge to add this functionality to our website page. Working closely with the developer teams on this was crucial to ensure it all worked.
- The luxury perfume advert – from the beginning of the campaign, we were keen to find a way to use our new YouTube Director, Rory Reid, in the creation of content. For those who don't know him, Rory is a former Top Gear presenter and is now responsible for the content on our YouTube channel. Having a recognisable personality as the 'face of the fragrance' helped add some style to our spoof, luxury perfume ad. This was produced entirely in-house and was shot in a cinematic style, with Rory performing a self-penned rap about the 'smell of success'. This was posted across all of AutoTrader's organic social-media channels and promoted across paid channels too.
- The mockumentary – in addition to the 'luxury' ad, we created a number of follow-up videos in a hilarious mockumentary-style, showing behind-the-scenes footage of Rory creating the scent. This gave us more content that we were able to promote across social media and the Eau de New Car landing page.
- The billboard – in a first for AutoTrader, we also placed 'scented' billboards in major shopping centres throughout the UK. These not only displayed the perfume advert, but also automatically dispensed a blast of the fragrance to curious passersby.
- The coverage – we issued two press releases – a launch release, plus the news story revealing the results of our research regarding brand-new cars and how the British public associate the smell of success with the smell of a new car. We also worked closely with our agency to execute a number of morning interviews with a scent specialist, to provide commentary on why we love the smell of a new car.

- The email – in addition to social, paid and organic channels, we also used our email database to send opted-in users a marketing email that directed them to the landing page and showcased the video.

We're incredibly proud of this campaign, not least because of the results, but also the level of collaboration between our teams. There's a tendency in SEO teams to remain siloed and narrowly focused on what we are doing day-to-day. But we learned that having conversations with multiple teams, asking questions and generally influencing others is key to success.

The question of 'control' versus 'influence' is not a new one, but it's an important one to understand if you want to achieve things here. As in-house SEOs, the degree to which we control things will vary massively, so it's important to recognise where and how you can influence.

This campaign was a perfect example of where the SEO team had a relatively low level of control (budgets, decisions, execution), but a high degree of influence (hiring of the agency, naming of the campaign, the landing page, creative input).

SMELL BY NUMBERS

Some of the key performance highlights of the campaign:

- Rankings for the core target keyword 'new car deals' increased from page two-to-three to floating between position two-to-four on the first page of Google. Our target was to achieve a page one ranking.
- The Eau de New Car campaign gained 394 links from 169 referring domains – 146 of these links were secured by our agency from high-authority publications. Our target was a minimum of 90.

- Unique pageviews for our relevant 'new car' landing pages increased by 23 percent – our target was to increase by 10 percent.
- New car ad views (how many times an ad for a new car was viewed on AutoTrader) increased by roughly 8.5 percent – our target was to increase by 5 percent – and although this may sound small, we are talking about tens of millions of views.
- New car leads (how many times a user interacts with a new car ad, such as sending an enquiry) increased by 173 percent – our target was to increase by 20 percent.
- 89 percent key message penetration in our coverage (coverage mentioning new car) – our target was 80 percent
- The campaign achieved 2.8 million impressions across social channels – our target was 2 million.
- The campaign won two awards at the 2020 UK Search Awards for Best Use of PR in a Search Campaign and Best Use of Search - Automotive.

WHY EDUCATION IS KEY TO SUCCESS

KEVIN WILES

GROUP SEO MANAGER, HALFORDS

Kevin, who's based in Stratford upon Avon, is the Group SEO Manager at high-street outdoors giant Halfords, where he applies his experience in helping businesses grow their online exposure, increasing revenue, traffic and overall keyword visibility.

He also has deep familiarity with key CMS platforms such as Shopify, WordPress, Magento, OpenCart and Salesforce Cloud Commerce.

At Halfords, I have learned a great deal about being an effective in-house SEO, particularly the importance of building relationships with, and getting wider buy-in from, other teams.

Specifically, I led a multisite website migration – helping Halfords combine two different customer bases and two different websites into one digital platform – which is the Halfords website you see today.

Before this, our traditional retail site Halfords.com and Halfords Autocentres, which is our garage and MOT operation, were on two separate domains. They were combined with one sole purpose – to deliver a better end-to-end solution for customers.

When we decided to merge the two, I shifted from just managing the retail .com website to also managing and incorporating all the Autocentre content, along with the technical nuances of the business.

We learned very quickly that this would need to be driven by a new strategy and process.

MAKING SEO A COMMERCIAL PRIORITY

You soon learn as an in-house SEO that it's one thing having a plan, a backlog of content ready to go live and JIRA tickets for site-speed improvements – but it's another thing to actually get those elements done.

While there is never a shortage of SEO amends and desirables that can be made to a website, not every business has the luxury of implementing all of these elements. You need to start small and pick a few things where you can show a direct impact.

A lot of the time, the list of business changes and requests is huge, and can result in SEO being pushed below other commercial priorities. My challenge was to help the business understand the sheer opportunity of SEO and the commercial impact it can have, both within our website migration, but also during a global pandemic.

Although I knew our plan and strategy was robust, I needed to comprehensively show the business how SEO could support us in reducing paid-media spend, identifying COVID-related terms and reducing customer-service contacts, which have an operational cost.

A large part of this is about getting an understanding of other teams' KPIs to see how SEO can align to these and, as a result, get wider buy-in.

And the biggest challenge here wasn't that anyone was doing anything wrong, it was that they were all working to different KPIs. So I put time into understanding the KPIs of the merchandising team, versus how the sprint teams worked. As the SEO, I needed to spend time understanding their psychology and motivation.

If you need new pages developed, you go to the front-end developers. If you want the site speed to improve, that sits within a development sprint release. That team is being pulled in all directions, on other business projects, that are all also seen as top priority.

As soon as you can understand different pain points within different business units internally, you can tweak your agenda to be more aligned with that stakeholder, meaning you're more likely to get traction.

You're no longer going to be seen as saying 'the SEO team needs this to drive X number of incremental visits or sales'. It's about saying 'if we improve the efficiency of your category pages, we can support you against your X, Y and Z metrics'.

Suddenly, the perception of SEO changes to be something that can support their work, rather than them supporting yours.

GETTING SMART DURING COVD-19

During the pandemic, our work was all about supporting the customer to get products and answers to common questions as quickly as possible, which allowed the business to maintain scale and customer service during a period of massive uncertainty.

We saw a huge increase in the amount of customer contacts being made to our support teams around opening hours, product-stock levels, delivery times and more. And in internal meetings, we were made aware of this increase, which was resulting in more people being needed to handle the volume of calls.

However, for me as an SEO, the thought was 'what if we could use that data and our tools, such as Also Asked, to do a better job of answering those online through informational content or PDPs that would reduce calls to the support centre?'. Our job as an SEO is to solve problems like this with data that we have direct from customers and Google.

In terms of technology and processes, we changed our approach to those things completely. We had to forget the big projects we wanted to do, because the developers were busy doing 'click and collect', or in-store pick-up and adapting to the new Covid messaging.

So we shifted our whole approach to focus on things like internal linking, scaling pages, putting new processes in place and creating flow diagrams for teams to follow.

I think SEOs sometimes like to squirrel away in a corner, but that just tells the business we're weird and quirky, and they leave us alone. It has to be the opposite if you want in-house SEO to be a success. You have to get as many people as possible saying, 'have you checked that with SEO yet?'.

KEEP BEING SMART

And you need to keep showing that SEO is not there to add a step in anyone's process or delay things. If anything, you're there to make things faster, because you have access to tools that allow the business to scale.

SEO teams can use a tool like DeepCrawl to crawl the company's website at scheduled intervals when the business is releasing new content, across both staging and live environments. The developers can't do that and have no way of checking these things. This might not directly impact SEO, but you're helping people and building networks.

Another example of a useful activity that isn't technically part of SEO is helping set content live. If you have content ready to go, ask the front-end developers for templates that you can drop it into, so that you can give them back the actual HTML and the code they need to upload.

You're helping with their workload, and that's very easy for technical SEOs, because we have the skills and knowledge to get those things done. Don't just sit there and assume that the SEO is only there to do keyword research. Empower the teams that are putting the products online, or creating content, to have access to your great tools so they can get that data themselves.

If I had to sum all this up, I would say that there is no one silver bullet that makes all this really easy. It was a case of doing the basics as well as we could and putting processes in place at a much faster pace. Then it's about getting involvement from other teams across the business. Something seems to have worked, as Halfords is now the number one for search items in the cycling space.

Picking these small battles and projects to demonstrate how useful SEO can be is the best basis for building useful work networks. Cracking this challenge involved technology – but also communication. The reality is that you need to put in work to build relationships, they're critical.

WHAT THEY DON'T TELL YOU ABOUT THE DOING IN-HOUSE VERSUS AGENCY

A lot of SEOs think the job is pretty much the same whether you are working for an agency or in-house. You're still going to be doing SEO, surely? In truth, it's never that simple.

When you're in an agency, you're focused on client deliverables. You have to deliver a specific project or report, or audit or whatever. What I've seen is that in-house is actually about my understanding of all the other teams' KPIs, building relationships that help educate them on SEO and meeting their goals.

You have to respect that your new colleagues are people that have trained in their own specialist fields and are very good at what they're doing. Therefore, they don't necessarily understand what you're talking about when you bring up canonicals and duplicate product pages and all those kinds of things!

But if you slot in, and see that your role is fundamental in helping them achieve their KPIs, you'll be fine.

HOW KNOWING YOUR TERMS CAN HELP YOU WIN FRIENDS AND INFLUENCE PEOPLE

DAVID WILLIAMS

SENIOR SEO MANAGER, JELLYFISH

David has worked in a wide range of agency roles over more than a decade in SEO, with the last seven years spent working in-house for large ecommerce brands.

Now, this particular ecommerce specialist is flourishing in an in-house role for UK retail giant Matalan, relishing the opportunity to focus all his energy on one website, helping one brand.

At time of interview David was SEO Lead at Matalan

I joined Matalan back in 2018 as SEO manager, but at the time, the SEO team didn't actually have any voice outside of the ecommerce traffic team, and only had a budget for a few tools.

That wasn't what you would expect for the size of the business and the importance of the channel.

The story of how I changed the brand's internal knowledge of SEO, and grew the channel's, and my credibility, is an interesting one – and SEO now plays a role in all aspects of the business.

When I looked at Matalan before joining, I was impressed with how big the brand was, but I had a sense it was underachieving in SEO.

Once I was onboard and able to dive into the data, I saw there wasn't a lot of change going on for the channel – there was a backlog of IT tickets and it had very little influence on any website changes or the business at large. This was something I could see was having an impact on year-on-year growth, which was slowing down.

My key challenges were to increase the presence of SEO in the business, and use it to improve our traffic and sales. But from an SEO perspective, it was how to do this without an SEO team or any agency support.

I could see that I was going to need help, due to the sheer size of the website. So the way I tried to tackle this was to secure buy-in from all areas of the business – and quickly.

FINDING THE FACTS ON 'LEISURE WEAR' VERSUS 'LOUNGEWEAR'

I was lucky to form a very useful alliance in my early days at the business – a colleague who joined Matalan at the same time as me, who was in charge of the men's department.

The department was struggling to meet its targets and was seen to be underperforming, so I proposed we work together to turn that around – and because she was also new to the business, she was willing to try new things.

We reviewed the men's category and tried to understand why it was struggling. I started with keyword research to understand what terms we were targeting – and if they were the right ones for products, categories and in the navigation.

I am convinced starting a project like this with keyword research is key – search data shows you the volume in the market, seasonality, growth of terms, and the difference between what we call something as a brand, versus what our customers actually search for.

What you tend to find is that certain departments have an opinion on what a product or category should be called. But, using Google search data, you can share information that isn't based on opinion but fact, as well as showing things like products that we consider to be seasonal, but actually have large volumes all year around.

What did this look like in practice? I got all the information for the men's department and examined names for specific categories. At that time, Matalan had a category called 'leisure wear', which got 44,000 searches, and which we changed to 'loungewear' – because that gets 1.4 million. If you name your category without this kind of information, you may be targeting a term that's got significantly less traffic.

Interestingly, the leisure wear versus loungewear issue was found after I trained an industry placement student on the basics of keyword research – showing that anyone can make a difference to a large business.

Another great example of this is a category we had within the navigation based on early research called 'suit trousers'. 'Suit trousers' had 146,000 searches a year, but the buying team wanted to change the term to 'formal trousers,' which only had 26,000.

Once I showed them this data, and other big opportunities that they didn't know existed, I was able to work with them on the next season's products and even increase our category options.

The key for me was increasing SEO's influence, and quickly, and part of this was about training other departments to use this information themselves, such as the trading team and the team that add products to the website.

For this, we used Google Keyword Planner, which many SEOs use to provide you with insight into the volume for terms over the last 12 months. We used this alongside Google Search Console (GSC), which shows terms that customers searched for in order to find the Matalan website.

I did, however, control the information being shared with other departments, as if it is not used correctly, it could give you the wrong information.

REVEALING THAT SEO WAS OUR BIGGEST SALES CHANNEL

Based on my findings, I did a presentation to senior management to show them the way to restart our growth. I defined SEO for them, talked about how big it was within the business and how much revenue it drives, not only online but in store.

I also pointed out that there were search terms out there with real volume in the market that we weren't taking full advantage of.

It was a real eye-opener for this audience, because they just hadn't realised that SEO was Matalan's biggest sales channel, along with driving more than double the amount of new customers than its closest channel.

Now they understood why it was so vital that we focussed on this channel for business growth.

After that, things moved pretty rapidly. Inside five months, the men's department went from underperforming to being the fastest growing after women's. This attracted the interest of other departments, who started coming to me to see how we could replicate this success.

And this is how, just using search data from a part of the business that was struggling, and showing how to turn things around, I ended up influencing the whole business. Not just the trading, and buying and merchandising, teams, but also point-of-sale, content and the team that produce the mailer. To increase the brand presence in Google, I needed to align us all.

KEEP YOUR EYE ON TRENDS – AND KIM KARDASHIAN

Sometimes other departments will say, 'that's what x brand would call it' and I have to gently remind them that it doesn't mean they're right. That brand could have just copied the wording from another brand, and maybe we're all wrong and not using the best term.

I'm sure it's the same in any big business – especially ones that have grown through bricks and mortar stores – and are in the early stages of online growth. Buyers want to call it 'this', the marketing team thinks it should be called something else. What I found myself constantly saying was, 'it's not me making up these terms – this is what our customers searched for, so we really should align behind that'.

It's important to remember that, if there is an inconsistency with what we call an item of clothing online, versus what we're calling it in our stores, if the customer can't find it on the website, we've lost a sale.

There's also a close link between search terms and brand. If your brand is well-known and there's a lot of brand searches for 'Matalan X', Google notices that, just another reason why optimising your product naming is so important to an ecommerce business. You must use the best name that search data gives you.

I also try to be proactive and helpful beyond this work. At one point, one of my team noticed a spike in search impressions in GSC for 'embroidered bomber jacket', around the time Kim Kardashian had been wearing an expensive version that was covered in The Daily Mail. So we immediately alerted our buyers – and we sold out. Now this isn't possible for most businesses, I know, but where you can, this should be a tactic for new trends.

I know a lot of the SEO industry knows what I've covered here, but I think what's key to this is that not everyone in the rest of the business does.

For those just starting out in SEO – remember – the data is there, you access it on a daily basis, so don't be afraid to use it to drive improvements in the business.

Start by targeting one initial opportunity – and once you win there – you'll quickly gain credibility and attention across the organisation.

WILL SEO END UP BEING AUTOMATED?

There is a lot of automation already in the industry, in both established and new SEO tools, which gather a wide range of data from onsite and offsite factors. The key to having access to this data is knowing how you can make it actionable.

Over the last year I've become more aware of the programming language Python for SEO automation, for instance, which has been driven by the amazing Hamlet Batista.

But there are still a lot of aspects of SEO that can't be automated. Human checks are still required to make sure decisions are right.

There are also so many different types of businesses, all at different stages of growth and maturity, on different platforms, which all have different capabilities.

So I predict we will always need SEOs and developers to help fix things, adapt to change, and seize opportunities.

YOU'RE RESPONSIBLE FOR A LARGE PROPORTION OF SALES AT ANY LARGE COMPANY – GET THE TECHNICAL SKILLS AND EMBRACE IT

NICK WILSDON

CONSULTANT, VODAFONE

SEO was about trying to open the 'black box' of Google when Nick Wildson joined the digital industry. Two decades on, he is an experienced marketer and strategist with a particular expertise in cross-platform campaigns.

Nick is passionate about digital performance, integrated campaigns and generally joining up the dots. With a proven track record in everything from digital strategy to affiliate marketing and more, he shares his insights from working for one of the world's biggest brands.

I've been an embedded consultant at Vodafone for the past eight years, and it's such a huge enterprise (560 million mobile customers across 22 markets) that establishing myself, and demonstrating the value of SEO, has been a brilliant challenge.

I see my main strength in SEO on the technical side. That's important because I have become increasingly convinced that it's next to impossible for external agencies to be effective at working with a large brand when it comes to technical SEO.

It just has to be done in-house, because you're dealing with so many issues across so many websites, as well as so many internal teams. However enthusiastic or skilled an agency might be, they struggle to make the levers move in a big organisation.

Over the last few years, Vodafone has relied less and less on agencies for strategy and for leadership, and instead we only lean on them as resources to help us conduct specific tasks. That perspective shapes how I see SEO – and how I think it can make a difference.

FROM REACTION TO EXPERIMENTATION

It's very easy when you're in-house to be reactive. You're probably the entirety of the SEO function, or you might have a very small team. Often, you don't have a lot of resources – so when people around the business come to you and say – 'I need this to work better in Google', then that's what you direct all your energy into.

The problem with that is that you're never pushing your own agenda for SEO. You're always assisting on other people's projects.

It's important that you try to take a step back and think of the SEO agenda.

How are you going to plan your SEO idea to make a programme that's as effective as possible? That doesn't mean you sit around doing nothing. A good SEO needs to be constantly experimenting and researching changes in the market. That's what we used to call 'building proofs of concept', or what McKinsey refers to as a constant 'test and learn' loop.

In practice, this means you're going to keep doing the necessary 'business as usual' SEO. But you should also be running a very active testing and learning stream on the side. I'm running experiments all the time, which is how I picked up on new things like Schema very quickly.

If you're working with international markets, you may well have a smaller one that's keen to try new things. Try your new thing there, then build a business case for rolling it out at scale for the business.

A good in-house SEO is someone who has the ability to do this, because it only counts if you land it. In-house SEOs have almost a greater responsibility to get these things working, because they have to see them through from planning, to execution, to the retrospective.

THE RISE OF THE TECHNICAL SEO

Technical SEO has been on the rise now for 10 years, but it's really sped up in the last five.

Today, it's still a very separate and different element. In some respects, the SEO discipline has almost become too wide. It's hard for people to define what it is, because it might be the person who creates content, it might be the person who's doing outreach, it might even be the person who's working with the development team to improve your CMS.

But I think the best in-house SEO today is now the technical one. The reason for that is because technical SEOs are the ones best placed to deal with the big problems that brands are facing online. It may be that the website architecture is wrong. It may be that there are lots of key parts of the site on sub-folders that are not aggregating into the website. These are really large, structural problems for brands.

To be successful as an in-house SEO, you have to really embrace the technical and work out how to develop a long-term strategy to deal with the big issues. If you don't, all you're going to be dealing with are peripheral things and you're never going to be let loose to deal with what you know is holding the site back.

This seems like a lot of work, but there's a great reason to adopt this model of thinking, strategically, while testing and learning. Whatever anyone might tell you, SEO is the basis for a very large percentage of sales at any large company.

Sales usually come from a combination of organic, paid media and direct, which means that SEO is always going to be one of the top-three channels. You will probably need to do some evangelising internally to have senior leaders recognise this fact, and to dispel the notion that Google somehow gives us this for free. It's definitely something we need to put the work in to improve.

I find it useful to educate people about the difference between brand and generic traffic. Large brands have huge amounts of brand traffic and they will always get traffic from Google because a brand name like 'Vodafone' is relevant to many searches.

The real challenge comes when you need to prove you can do better and win generic traffic. That's when you start taking away traffic and potential sales from the competition.

YOUR POWERS IN PRACTICE

For the last six months, I've been working with an international telecoms provider on these issues. It was a technical SEO project and our initial goal was to improve the indexing of material on their site. A lot of the content wasn't visible to Google, so wasn't getting crawled or indexed.

To do this, we worked very closely and successfully with the development team – and this is very typical of where SEO is moving – working with technical teams to make useful changes. We managed to fix a lot of issues with the CMS and make the content more readable by Google. And I'm happy to say we saw a significant upswing in traffic and rankings, just with that one step.

I'm also a huge fan of Schema deployment, which is a way of marking up information on a webpage that relates back to the Semantic Web work that Tim Berners-Lee created. Google has really taken Schema on board quite strongly, and now more than 50 percent of its search features are powered by it. I recommend that all SEOs become familiar with it.

In this instance, I found Schema useful as a way to mark up information on the website so that Google would 'see' the relationship between all our products. If I'm selling an iPhone X, I can mark that up so Google knows it's an Apple product, it runs iOS, what memory it has and size it is. All of these separate, handy bits of information can be connected with Schema.

We did well on this project because I have a strong technical understanding of JavaScript, SEO and Schema. A good SEO is someone who is constantly learning and exercising their curiosity. If you're not pushing yourself to test and learn, you'll stagnate, even if you're a senior SEO, you still need to be testing and learning to expand your knowledge.

It also came down to that strategic way of thinking that I'm constantly striving for as an in-house SEO. If you want to be really good, you need to be the person who can see big-picture problems and is thinking about these large, structural issues, and has the ability to deal with immediate opportunities.

Finally, you need to have the insight into how to support the business to make those big changes. It's very hard for an external agency to deliver all of this, which is why in-house SEO is so important. External agencies can do a lot of things that are really useful, but don't necessarily address the big issues. This is why you can, and should, embrace technical SEO as your best way to win big at the next stage in your career.

And the even better news? It's a lot of fun.

IF YOU WANT SEO TO BE TAKEN SERIOUSLY IN THE BOARDROOM – LEARN THE ART OF GETTING THINGS DONE

Even though SEO is growing in status and I think we're heading into a boom time – it's still not always taken seriously by the c-suite.

Currently, 40 percent of retail sales in the UK happen online excluding groceries. These sales are dictated in many cases by SEO. But this contribution and success isn't being recognised at the top of the organisation.

Of course, that doesn't mean you should start complaining that 'SEO isn't taken seriously', so if you're tempted to say this – stop.

Are you approaching the business in a way that would make them take you seriously? What are the projects that you're proposing? What's your plan? Are you working on your relationships with senior management to help you convey what you're trying to do?

I don't think SEOs always understand the value of planning – and if you want SEO to be taken seriously as a channel, you need to plan it seriously. Look at how successful consultants and top-line management consultancies work, and you'll see planning is something they spend a lot of time on. It's something that they charge clients for.

More often than not, the role of an in-house SEO at a senior level is to get management to understand the value of SEO so that resources are allocated to it.

Otherwise, it's always going to be a very hard thing to secure. I think it's useful to think about this as the art, of the politics, of SEO, or the art of getting things done.

HOW TO MAKE SEO A GENUINE GROUP EFFORT

MOSHE MA-YAFIT

SENIOR TECHNICAL SEO AT WIX

Just over a decade ago, a young man called Moshe saw a TV programme about how a kid like him was doing amazing things with something called SEO.

He's recently joined Wix as a Senior Tech SEO after working as SEO lead at Natural Intelligence, and has a proven history of working on big and complex websites, including at Ladbrokes in the UK.

Moshe sees his mission as boosting organic traffic for the brands he works with, and is passionate about sharing his knowledge to benefit the wider global SEO community.

This is the story of how I got buy-in to build and manage a huge, scalable 'Google Panda project' to get rid of all our low-quality content – all with the full support of our product, marketing, operations and development teams.

It's also the story of how I got some really neat things into our CMS, including a three-click way to implement 410 status codes on pages.

My journey began when I started my previous job at Natural Intelligence just before the first Covid lockdown. The company is a global leader in multi-vertical, online comparison marketplaces, so I knew I'd be doing a lot of interesting work – and I wasn't wrong.

If you're looking for the best meal delivery or dating service in the US, they can get you affiliated with the relevant partners for that product.

SEO is still very new for Natural Intelligence, so the first challenge I had was education. I certainly didn't mind that, because I love SEO education.

I also love taking a company that's new to SEO and building great SEO from scratch.

A PROBLEM WITH AUTHORITY

Having no SEO at all was a huge challenge when I arrived. Natural Intelligence focuses on comparison websites in both Europe and in the US market, but in the US, they operate across more than 50 verticals, everything from psychic readings to the best VPNs.

This meant Natural Intelligence had a very complex website – and I don't need to tell any in-house SEOs that this presents a big challenge for us – because authority-wise, it is very hard to show Google that you are relevant for so many different topics.

My tried and tested response is to take a bottom-up strategy. This means, if I want to implement something cross-company, I don't start by approaching line managers.

Let me give an example. When I started this job, I could see right away that we needed to upgrade our technology stack. The developers were working with a horrible old Javascript library, Zepto, and I immediately started to work with them and push for a move to React. That's a big change, not just for SEO, but for the entire company.

My bottom-up strategy was that I went to developers and the PPC team and the UX people – to get their support for this change. I needed to make it clear to each community in the company why React would be so much better for them.

For example, developers couldn't really develop seriously with this older library, because it doesn't support modern capabilities. For the marketing people, I pointed out that if we had a better technology stack, we could do much more sophisticated testing and bring success to the company.

If I got the support of fellow employees, I'm demonstrating the value of them doing what I want them to do, and they will start to ask their managers to get it. Then I will demonstrate the value of the change at company decision-maker level, by bringing numbers, and explaining what it can do in terms of user experience, which is very important right now.

MAKING BETTER CONTENT A COMPANY ISSUE

The Google Panda algorithm was supposed to target low-quality content. That sounds simple, but like the library change, it would need the whole company behind it if we really wanted to improve our content.

The first step in my project was internal education. I created an SEO course for the whole company and ran it for 30 people at a time. In it, we gave everyone a presentation about the basics of SEO, so people could understand fundamentally what it is.

This was so effective that once the Panda work started, people were coming to us unprompted, because they understood what a canonical tag was, and they could see for themselves that their page wasn't indexed. The entire company became our agents of change.

Based on measures and KPIs from Google Search Console, Semrush and other tools, we collated multiple useful KPIs that showed us the visits, traffic and revenue created by each page.

We then manually reviewed each one – and we talked about Panda and what low-quality content looks like. We also gave people a decision tree to help them understand if a page was low-quality, so for each page, we could use that to decide to leave it alone, improve the content, consolidate it, or remove it. We used the decision tree to assess thousands of pages.

Developers really got into this spontaneously and helped us by writing a 410-status code. This is to tell Google not to index a specific page – and we added a function to our CMS that let the content team flag a page with this 410-status. Now, in three clicks, I can remove a page from the CMS and tell Google the page should be removed from search results.

GENUINE COLLABORATION

In parallel, we worked with the content team to improve our content. We did really comprehensive keyword and competitor research, data analysis and so on.

We also worked closely with the PPC team to make sure we never removed pages they were using. We coordinated everything with all the marketing channels, operation teams and anyone else who needed to be involved.

For example, I have weekly meetings with the product team to make sure we are fully aligned. We need to know where the files are, where the support tickets are, and everything has to be recorded.

We make sure that when we create or change any task, feature or widget, the product people know about it. They know what our motivation is in making this request, and how it's going to increase traffic, revenue, or both.

All of this enabled us to massively improve the quality and authority of the website. We are moving very quickly away from any danger of Google not seeing our content, or not seeing it as high-enough quality for users.

Genuine collaboration and buy-in is so important for making in-house SEO a success. Education is also critical, because if you can motivate colleagues to help with SEO, you get better results.

You can motivate people by letting them learn something that they don't know, showing how you can contribute to their work or by improving their general knowledge. People are people – and it's natural to think this might be something they can take to another company when they move on.

WHAT MAKES A REALLY EFFECTIVE IN-HOUSE SEO?

SEOs tend to think we know everything. We might know a lot, but we don't really know why.

SEO is all about assumptions. The difference between SEO now, versus 15 years ago, is that 15 years ago, it was 90 percent deterministic, and 10 percent probabilistic. Today, the opposite is true.

I am really humble when I talk to people. When I talk to engineering – I need to remember that they know how to code a lot better than me. Yes, I've developed apps in Java, and I am building automation tools in Python, but that is very little compared to their knowledge.

It's always better to approach people with an attitude of, 'I think we can help each other and I'd be so grateful for...'.

Remembering this keeps me personally focussed. I keep reminding myself that the SEO game keeps changing and if you come with this attitude, then people will want to connect with you, to learn from you.

Humility is a key attribute for anyone who wants to be successful in SEO. I think we also need to know how to use certain situations to push through major improvements. We had a crisis in which traffic dropped by 30 percent for a few weeks, but we took that as a chance to improve things that hadn't been prioritised before. We blended several projects that were stuck in the backlog and explained that this needs to be done now.

A lot of the time, you need to be creative in how you justify SEO. Creativity is important in lots of ways. And I believe we all need to get a lot more creative in how we bring organic traffic to websites.

ABOUT BLUE ARRAY

We stand for SEO.

From the day we launched in early 2015, we've been pioneering a unique hybrid of agency and consultancy, we call this a 'consulgency'. It's an approach that allows us to give our clients the individual attention they need with the scale of an agency.

Never having taken investment, we have bootstrapped our way to over 50 employees, multi-million pounds of turnover, believing in SEO and its power to take businesses such as heycar, RAC and Pret to places they never thought possible.

We are an agency defining an industry, by putting purpose ahead of profit, turning obsession into drive, and using knowledge to educate.

Our mission is to elevate our people, customers and industry through SEO and use our business to positively influence a better world.

Find out more about us at bluearray.co.uk

SIMON SCHNIEDERS

Founder

Printed in Great Britain
by Amazon

65650414R00132